Give Yourself Permission to Shine

Give Yourself Permission to Shine

Shine

Through Faith I Found Love

Grace King

BALBOA
PRESS

A DIVISION OF HAY HOUSE

ISBN: 978-1-4525-4868-5 (sc)
ISBN: 978-1-4525-4869-2 (hc)
ISBN: 978-1-4525-4867-8 (e)

Balboa Press books may be ordered through booksellers or by contacting:

Balboa Press
A Division of Hay House
1663 Liberty Drive
Bloomington, IN 47403
www.balboapress.com
1-(877) 407-4847

Because of the dynamic nature of the Internet, any web addresses or links contained in this book may have changed since publication and may no longer be valid. The views expressed in this work are solely those of the author and do not necessarily reflect the views of the publisher, and the publisher hereby disclaims any responsibility for them.

Library of Congress Control Number: 2012904369

The author of this book does not dispense medical advice or prescribe the use of any technique as a form of treatment for physical, emotional, or medical problems without the advice of a physician, either directly or indirectly. The intent of the author is only to offer information of a general nature to help you in your quest for emotional and spiritual well-being. In the event you use any of the information in this book for yourself, which is your constitutional right, the author and the publisher assume no responsibility for your actions.

Any people depicted in stock imagery provided by Thinkstock are models, and such images are being used for illustrative purposes only.
Certain stock imagery © Thinkstock.

Printed in the United States of America
Balboa Press rev. date: 3/28/2012

For everyone who yearns to love themselves and to be connected to life's true purpose.

Through pain and suffering the path to enlightenment is lit and the door to experiencing true love, peace and joy is opened.

1 Corinthians 13:4-7

"Love is patient, love is kind. It does not envy, it does not boast, it is not proud. It is not rude, it is not self-seeking, it is not easily angered, it keeps no record of wrongs. Love does not delight in evil but rejoices with the truth. It always protects, always trusts, always hopes, and always perseveres."

Dictionary.com

bulimia bu·lim·i·a (by&oomacr;-līm′ē-á, -lē′mē-á, b&oomacr;-)

n   ·

A chronic eating disorder involving repeated and secretive episodes of eating, characterized by uncontrolled rapid ingestion of large quantities of food over a short period of time, followed by self-induced vomiting, purging, and anorexia and accompanied by feelings of guilt, depression, or self-disgust. Also called *binge-eating syndrome, bulimia nervosa or hyperorexia.*

Chapter 1

I REMEMBER THE MOMENT WHEN I first realized that I was bulimic. I was in my mother's house, in the bathroom, and I had just made myself vomit my food down the basin drain and quickly pushed it down with running water. I felt both excitement and fear. I had just started a new chapter in my life, but I had no true idea of what I was getting myself into. I was sixteen years old.

I am now thirty-four, and I have been recovered since December 19, 2003, just over nine years. I have had one relapse, after miscarrying my first baby. I am telling my story, and sharing my victory, with the hope that I may help someone who is going through what I went through. If I can reach out to help one person, then my pain and suffering would have been worth it. Please note that some of the information in this book may be triggering, but it is not intended to be harmful in any way.

I'll begin with sharing some background on my childhood. I was born and raised in Johannesburg, South Africa. I was an only child, raised by my mother. My memories of childhood are filled with an abundance of love, especially from my mother, my grandmother and grandfather, my aunties and cousins. However, there was also a subconscious sadness; a sadness that I would have denied. I never knew my father. Not by choice. He chose not to know me. When he found out my mother was pregnant, at eighteen, he left her, as it would have disgraced his religion, and he was not willing to take responsibility. So my mother had me just before her nineteenth birthday.

I remember meeting him once; I must have been about two or three. I remember my mom getting us ready and prepared for this "big day." "You are going to meet your dad today," Mom said, so I put on my best dress and the house was in perfect order. I don't remember his face, although I do remember his presence. What I do remember is my mom and him talking, probably more like arguing. He took twenty rand out of his wallet, threw it on the table, and said, "Buy the child some food," and walked out. I never saw him again.

Growing up, I never really missed my dad. My mom was always very open and honest with me about him and what had happened and why he wasn't around. When I was ready, she would help me find him. I didn't feel a great need for him, as I had everything I needed: my mom, my grandma, my grandpa, and there was certainly never a shortage of love and affection in our family. Although there was, at times, a shortage of food and money.

As a young child, having a shortage of food and money didn't really matter to me, as I didn't understand what that meant. All I knew was that if I was hungry, there was something for me to eat, even if it was only a slice of bread or a bowl of pasta, and a glass of milk. I always had something to eat. Only as I got older and became more aware of what was going on did I realize that we had less than others in way of materialistic things, as well as much less food in our house. We very rarely could afford to go away on beach holidays or places outside of our home town.

Now I realize that being "money poor" in my childhood was a blessing in disguise. It has taught me the wonderful quality of gratitude, appreciation, and the humility of counting my blessings every day, for everything, big and small, in my life. My family and I were brought up knowing that even though we didn't have much, there was always someone else who had less than us, so we had a lot to be thankful for. We knew our greatest blessing was that we had each other. So perhaps you could say we were "poor in money" but we were "rich in love"!

Chapter 2

WHEN I WAS ABOUT NINE, I wrote my dad a letter. My mom always encouraged me to seek the truth and look for my dad when I was ready. I wrote to him to say that I wanted to meet him and get to know him as my dad, even if it was only one time, nothing more. I said I didn't want any money from him, just to look in his eyes and see what he looked like, so that at least I could say that I knew my father and so that I could identify with that part of me. Anyone that knew my dad, and had met me, always said that I looked so much like him. I wanted to see that too! I included a photo of myself in the letter. My mom posted it.

We went to the place my mom suggested we meet at, the Yugoslav Club, and we waited for hours. He never showed up. Later that week, my mother got a phone call from my dad. He said, "It was your fault you fell pregnant, she's your mistake, and I want nothing to do with her!" He sent the letter and the photos back to my mom. I can't really remember exactly how I felt, but I remember feeling disappointed. My mom always made me feel like it was his loss that he didn't want to be a part of my life. I never felt liked I "lacked" a dad, because I was so spoilt with an abundance of love from my mom and my family that it never seemed like he was missing. I must have numbed the pain.

There was a bizarre time when I met my dad's brother, Barto. My mom was angry at my dad for hurting me after he had sent my letter and photos back to her and after his phone call to my mom saying it was her mistake to have fallen pregnant and her decision to have kept me, so my mom decided to be hard with him. After all, he had not taken any responsibility for me in any way. She filed for child support from him, only to discover that there was already another child support charge against him. He was ordered to appear in court to plead his case but he did not show up. A warrant went out for his arrest. The police served the warrant at his brother's work place by mistake. They had the same initials and obviously the same last name, so that is how the police made that mistake.

Uncle Barto told the police he wasn't sure where my dad was. He hadn't seen him in a long time. He would let them know if he turned up. He said he would be happy to call my mother and speak to her, as he felt he held some responsibility for his brother. My uncle had known about me through the grapevine. He called my mom and agreed to meet with me.

It was a strange day. I wasn't sure how I felt. My mom was excited that I was meeting Uncle Barto, but I really wasn't; he wasn't my dad, and my dad still did not want to meet me. We met Barto and his wife at a restaurant. His wife was German and didn't speak English. When Barto saw me, he gave me a big hug. I felt quite indifferent. Barto was not my dad. There seemed to be some confusion; Barto's wife seemed to think that I was Barto's child and that my mom and Barto had been lovers in the past. Apparently, according to her, I looked just like Barto. I remember my mom making quite the effort to explain to her that this was not the case, that I was Barto's brother's child, and that he did not want to know me, and so Barto had taken that responsibility on himself. She did not believe it. She was convinced I was Barto's child, she said the resemblance was too strong and she felt extremely hurt that she was sitting with my mom at the table, who she was totally convinced was at some point "the other woman." The language barrier was quite a challenge, and the whole experience was extremely emotional for everyone, except me.

Everyone was crying and in tears, holding hands and talking about me. I felt totally out of place. My dad still did not want to see me, and it was not my dad sitting at the table with me. I felt numb.

At the end of lunch, we all left the table and walked out of the restaurant. Barto hugged me and gave me his telephone number, saying that if I ever needed anything, I should call him. He also gave me fifty Rand. I said thank you and smiled, knowing I most probably would never call him. I never spoke to Uncle Barto or saw him again. I later found out about two years later, that he committed suicide. What a mystery; I wondered why he felt he couldn't cope with his life anymore and if I could've helped make a difference to his destiny.

In hindsight, I probably should have been more open to meeting my uncle; at least I would've known someone from my dad's side of the family. And who knows, if I had gotten close enough to Uncle Barto, perhaps I would've met my father. But at the time I was a stubborn teenager, who thought I knew what was best for me, and if it wasn't my dad I was getting to know, it didn't seem to matter. But I guess unfortunately now I will never know.

Looking back now, I realize that I carried a lot of pain from my dad's rejection and a lot of guilt about my dad leaving us. Although it still feels like I never felt the pain, as I was in denial about it most of my childhood, I must have felt it on a subconscious level. The feeling of rejection and abandonment only set in later on in my life. It developed into a fear of being rejected and abandoned. I still have not met my father, but I would really love to, to know him and make peace with him. Perhaps if I were to pray for him often enough, and find truth and acceptance in my need for him, perhaps our paths will cross one day. Maybe he yearns to meet me too. I can only hope that he will find hope and courage in his heart, and with that faith, he too can find his way to make amends with me, his daughter. Perhaps this book will somehow bring us together; who knows? Anything is possible!

I was very fortunate to have my wonderful grandparents in my life, especially throughout my childhood, who gave me lots of nurturing love and support. My grandma is very special to me, and we have always been very close. She has always shared her wisdom with me and taught me about patience and kindness and persistence. She has always been tender and loving and understanding. Then there was my granddad. He was actually not my biological grandfather; my grandmother had remarried, so he was my step-grandpa, but the only one I ever knew throughout my early childhood (my mom only found her biological father in her midthirties, when I was about fifteen). Since I was a baby, Grandpa was always there for me. He became the father figure I never had. He was not able to have any children of his own, so I became the daughter he never had. We had a very special and very close bond up until his death.

Chapter 3

I WAS ALWAYS A HIGH ACHIEVER at school. I got good grades, was a school prefect, excelled at sport, took part in school concerts, and was generally a good all-rounder. I loved sport and took part in tennis, netball, softball, and basketball. I never had a weight problem and had a very healthy appetite. Well, my appetite was quite huge actually; my mom used to joke with me and say that I could "eat most men under the table," quite an odd saying, but what she meant was that I often ate more than some grown men did. I had a fast metabolism and was fortunate enough that I could eat what I wanted and remained at a steady weight. I was quite a healthy eater, though, enjoyed my fruit and vegetables and whole grains, which made it easy. But looking back, I also realize that I was an emotional eater, which I still am today. I remember friends saying to me, "Gosh, you never stop eating," which in a way is still true today. I loved food (who doesn't?), and food was nourishment, but also "recreation," for want of a better word. So I became known for my big appetite.

There were two very specific times when I had overeaten and felt like my stomach was going to burst. One specific occasion, I was with my friend Brooke. She had joined me at a softball function, and there was always such a wonderful variety of tasty foods to try. And of course, I had to try them all! So I did, and by the end of the evening, I was in pain. Then Brooke suggested, no doubt wanting to end my complaining about how sore my stomach was from being so full, "Why don't you just stick your fingers down your throat and make yourself vomit? Then you'll feel better."

I said, "No, I can't do that." And I didn't. Not that night.

Another time, I was at school, and it was my class's turn to organize a cake and candy fundraiser, where we had to sell an assortment of treats to eat, like cakes and biscuits and sweets, and popcorn and hot dogs, that type of thing, to raise money for the school. Each class got a turn. When it's your class's turn, it's a tradition that there are some "added benefits" of organizing the sale: you get to taste many of the treats before they are sold. This particular day, my friend Maria and I had gone a little crazy and eaten way too many hot dogs and pieces of cake; we both complained about our bursting bellies. So Maria suggested, "Let's go stick our fingers down our throat." I said I couldn't do it, and she said, "We'll do it together." So off we went to the bathroom; she was in the cubicle next to me. I heard her doing it, succeeding. I tried but could not get my fingers down my throat far enough. I couldn't do it. Not that day.

Chapter 4

WHEN I WAS GROWING UP, I became friends with a girl named Charlie. We met at a corner shop, when I was about six years old; we lived in the same street. She was exceptionally beautiful. During our teenage years, everywhere we went, she would turn heads, and people would always comment on how beautiful she was. To me, she was beautiful, inside and out. We were best friends for all our childhood years; we were like sisters, we even pretended that we were cousins, and people believed us. We were family to us. I got used to all the boys wanting to be her boyfriend and just wanting to be my friend. That was understandable to me, she was certainly much prettier than me, and she had a small petite frame, with a slim body and big breasts, and she was very athletic too.

I don't think I understood the impact this would have on me later, though, that feeling of never being "good enough," feeling like I was always in her shadow. But we loved each other very much. At times I was envious of how beautiful and slim she was, and I often wished I could be like her, as she always got every boyfriend she wanted, and all the attention. But I was happy with me—most of the time. I had many "boy friends," whom I loved dearly and loved me back, and we had fun hanging out together. My mom always allowed my boyfriends to visit me at home, where she could get to know them too. I always loved that about her. Later in our high school years, Charlie left school and moved away from our town, and our friendship kind of faded for a while. We didn't see each other for some time. Our friendship returned for a few years and then dwindled again, and we lost contact for a few years.

I was very fortunate to have had many good friends in my life growing up. At school, I became very good friends with Kate, who moved to Melbourne, as her parents wanted to get away from our crime-infested country. I was emotionally destroyed by her leaving, but her family was extremely kind to me and flew me out to visit Kate in Australia for six weeks; it was the best vacation that I ever had. Kate and I are still very close friends today. She is my daughter's godmother.

At Kate's farewell party, I met a guy named Eric; he was about five years older than me. He kindly gave me a lift home that night from the party. We became best friends through my high school years. He was a bit crazy, but I loved him dearly. We did everything together. He became part of my family. He was like my big brother. I kept my bulimia from him for a long time, but it started to become obvious with my sickly, thin frame and huge portions I ate; it didn't add up. Eric confronted me about it and asked me if I was bulimic, but I denied it. He had also caught me stealing chocolate bars from his house. Our friendship took a lot of strain through my bulimic years, as I was not the person I had been before. I was lying and sneaking around and not taking care of myself, and in turn, my attitude toward others had changed. I was becoming more withdrawn all the time, and Eric did not like who I had become.

After about five years of our friendship, Eric came to my house in the middle of the night, drunk, to tell me he no longer wanted to be friends. I was devastated but tried not to show it. He said I had changed and that I was no longer the fun, happy, open, honest person I used to be; I had become deceitful, selfish, and withdrawn. He had tried but I was not willing to open up and be honest, and he had had enough. I remember him asking me if I thought he was only saying this because he was drunk, and I said yes. But I was in denial. I knew he was telling me the truth, but I didn't want to believe it. So I denied the truth and made myself believe that I had done nothing wrong and that he was just exaggerating. We never spoke again. I am deeply sorry for hurting Eric and destroying our friendship. I hope he can forgive me.

I had another friend, Mary J, who I'd met through my mom's boyfriend. Mary J lived in a commune house with him. She was a few years older than me, and she was wild and wonderful. We became good friends. She invited me to join her on a holiday down to the south coast to meet her family. We had a great time, except that my bulimic activities ruined our friendship. She had known that I was bulimic, but I had said that I was recovered, which she quickly discovered to be a lie since we spent two weeks together at her parents' house. I sneakily helped myself to food in the fridge and spent too much time in the toilet, making myself vomit the food up. It was obvious. Mary J was furious with me. I know she loved me, but I hurt her and her family. I destroyed her trust in me as well as our friendship. I am deeply sorry for that, and I hope that Mary J and her family can forgive me.

I am mentioning these cherished yet ruined friendships because it's important to realize that amazing people are sent into our lives; they love and care for us and can truly help us, but bulimia protests that. Bulimia sabotages intimate relationships with its deceit, lies, and manipulation. I deeply regret the hurt I caused these wonderful people, these sincere special friends I once had. In order for me to heal properly, I need to forgive myself for the hurt and pain I have caused others, and I hope and pray that they too will forgive me.

Chapter 5

WHEN I WAS ABOUT FIFTEEN YEARS old, I met a boy at a school play audition. His name was Ricky. He was a gorgeous guy, from a good conservative home. He had a bright smile, big brown eyes, a strong body, and a gentle nature. He was also a magnificent ballroom dancer and took part in competitions. We fell in love. We had a sweet, innocent, romantic young love. He was my first love. We were together for about a year.

Over the summer, he had to go overseas for a dancing competition, and he would be gone for a few weeks. I was fine with that. I was preparing for exams, so it was a good time. He was away for a couple for months. I missed him terribly. Then I heard he was coming back, as I had spoken with his parents. I don't know why, but I didn't call him. I wanted him to call me first. I was being stubborn. He did call, but things seemed a little different. Perhaps I was different. I was a bit abrupt, waiting for him to tell me how much he missed me; my ego wanted to feel inflated so was looking for attention, I guess. He did tell me he missed me and wanted to see me. But I wanted a more dramatic response. He picked up on my vibes and attitude, and he must have thought that I didn't love him anymore and that the time we spent apart had created distance between us. I was not going to show him how I really felt, that I had missed him like crazy and, if anything, loved him even more. I wanted him to show me that first. I was being stubborn.

A few days later, he called to say that it was obvious that things between us had changed. Perhaps it was better that we broke up. I was devastated! I was heart-broken. But there was no way I was going to let him know that. My ego was taking a stand, even though it felt destroyed. So again, more stubborn than ever, I said that was a good idea. Meanwhile, I thought my life was over. I felt responsible for what had happened. It was my fault for being so stubborn and not being open and honest about my feelings. I should've told him how much I loved him! I felt unbearable pain and guilt. I felt worthless and lost.

My Ouma (great-grandmother) used to visit with family throughout the year. She'd spend two or three months at a time with each family member. It was our turn to have her visit us. I was about sixteen years old. My Ouma and I were not very close, but we got on fine. I was going through a time that I guess could be called the "terrible teenage years," and I had little patience for old people. So this particular visit from Ouma was not a very enjoyable one for me, and probably not for her. I loved her dearly, and she certainly loved me very much. She gave me some very good advice, when she could catch my attention. I remember her sitting me down and telling me, "Remember one thing, my child, in life, you must always keep your dignity, without your dignity, you have nothing." They were wise words from an old woman. Sadly, I was not very interested in what she had to say, and I was impatient with her.

Her visit came to an end, and she went on to stay with the next family member. This arrangement worked well for her, as the family didn't want to put her in an old age home, as she was still fit and able and did not need special care, just the love of her family. But about two years later, she needed to go to an old aged home, as she was becoming fragile. It was a very difficult and sad decision for the family.

We got a call one day that she had been admitted to hospital, as she had terrible pain in her leg. They discovered she had gangrene, and it was spreading incredibly fast. They had to amputate her leg. We all went to hospital to see her. She was quite drugged up from the painkillers. I think she was in shock too. Within hours, the gangrene had spread to her other leg, and that leg needed to be amputated too. This was extremely traumatic for her. She had had enough. She waited to see my mom, whom she was closest to, and then she died.

It was an emotionally devastating experience for our family. I felt tremendous guilt for not having made peace with my Ouma before she died. I never told her how much she meant to me and that I loved her and longed for her old advice and wise conversations more than ever. I also felt tremendous guilt for not having spent those last precious moments with her at the hospital. Instead, while everyone was with her, I snuck away to eat and purge.

Chapter 6

I LOVE FOOD. WHO DOESN'T, RIGHT? Looking back to my childhood, I can see now that I "ate my emotions." I still do, to a certain extent, today. Food was my comfort. I am also a creature of habit. I was used to overeating, which became a habit. The feeling of always having to be "full" consumed me. I was always searching for that feeling. And since I wasn't getting it emotionally, I was self-medicating with food. As I grew older, in my teenage years, I was starting to become more body conscious, more aware of my body and how society dictated that it should look.

After my Ouma died, and Ricky and I broke up, I turned to food for comfort, as I always did. This time, I was carrying a lot of emotional guilt as well as food guilt around with me. I wanted to be thin and slim and sexy, maybe then Ricky would see me and want to get back together. I tried many diets but couldn't stick to them. I tried starving myself, which I achieved for a day or two, and then I would binge eat. I could not avoid food. I needed to be full. I couldn't be thin and eat as much as I did. So I considered vomiting my food up if I ate too much, as my friends had suggested.

The first few times were very difficult. It was quite traumatic. At first, I couldn't get my finger down my throat deep enough and it hurt. The gagging was unpleasant and uncomfortable. The food was too dry and too hard. But I persisted. Overeating became an insatiable hunger, and I did not want to pay the price for it. I did not want to take responsibility for my actions, I would not be fat. I'd rather make myself vomit and endure the pain than be fat.

For some time during my younger years, my mom had been overweight. She had battled with obesity for many years. I remember seeing the pain and suffering she went through. She was probably struggling more emotionally and psychologically than physically. But her physical abilities were hindered too. I did not want to end up like that. Perhaps I was embarrassed at times by her obesity. I just knew I never wanted to be fat like that. Subconsciously, I had developed a fear of being fat. I think I'd linked my mom's loneliness and depression to her being fat. Looking back, I can see that my mom probably ate her emotions too. My mom had a very traumatic childhood that she was battling to deal with during her twenties and thirties. At the same time, she had to raise me on her own. She didn't put herself first, she put me first, and so I can see how it must have been easy to turn to food and alcohol for comfort to ease and numb her own pain. She was scared too and crying out for help. I did not see that then. I do now.

I started to experiment with all sorts of foods, to see what worked better to purge. At the time, this was great fun. I was generally quite a healthy eater. I loved fruits and vegetables, whole grain breads, yogurt, and nuts, those types of foods, and only overindulged in cakes and sweets and crisps on special occasions. My mom had brought me up that way. It was a new world to me, to indulge in these unhealthy treats, oily, sugar-filled, and salty foods. These seemed to work best. I could eat whatever I wanted to, and as much as I liked, with no "fat consequences." I thought I had found the perfect solution to a happy life. Eating became a hobby, and bulimia became my new best friend. Food no longer served me as nourishment, but simply "entertainment" to my taste buds, as often and as much as I wanted. Finally, I felt happy. At first it started out with one meal here and one meal there, where I'd have the second helping of dinner. Then I'd have an extra helping of dessert. No one thought much of it, as it was pretty much what I used to do anyway. But soon I started to brag about how much I had eaten. So it started to become more obvious at every meal. Family and friends started to notice and comment on how much I ate. I felt special. I loved the attention, hearing "How can you eat so much and be so thin?" Family, friends, and school peers started to become suspicious when I started losing weight. I was oblivious to their awareness of me and what I was doing. I continued on my journey in my "new and exciting world," bingeing and sneaking off to purge whenever I could.

Chapter 7

M Y SCHOOL WAS THE FIRST PLACE people suspected something was wrong. The sister of one of my peers was bulimic, and she recognized the signs in me. I denied it. Someone from my school phoned my grandfather and told him they suspected that I was bulimic. I denied it again. Then my principal, Mrs. Johnson, called me in to tell me that she had sincere concerns about me and my bulimia, as a teacher had spoken with her about her concerns that I was bulimic. She also had reports from other students.

I played tennis with one teacher from my school on the weekends. We played at her club and had cold drinks and snacks afterward. One time I had gone to the bathroom after we had eaten, and I was in there, making myself vomit, for some time. So she came in to see if I was okay. I walked out the cubicle saying I was fine and everything was okay. I'm certain she could smell the vomit on my breath; my eyes were red and watery. It would have been obvious, although I did not think so at the time. She was concerned and told my principal about it.

This was one of the first times I had admitted to it, in Mrs. Johnson's office. She wanted me to get professional help straight away. She called my mother in to tell her. I was devastated. This was my secret, no one was meant to find out, especially my mother. I did not want to disappoint her. I was always her high achiever, her star, her "perfect" child. My mother was shattered. She did not want to believe it. Mrs. Johnson suggested that I be sent away, to a special institution where they dealt with eating disorders. She said that she'd seen many girls in previous schools who had the same illness as me, and that if we didn't get professional help straight away, it could take me years, if ever, to be cured of this illness, as it is much harder when you take it into your adult life.

I was scared. I think my mom was terrified. She immediately said there was no way that I was being sent away. She would deal with it, with me, at home, together, under her supervision. I was also in my final year of school, and I did not want to jeopardize not finishing my final exams and getting the chance to matriculate with "A" grades, so that I stood a chance at going to university. While Mrs. Johnson understood my concerns about my final year, she did not think we were making the best decision. We didn't understand the nature of the beast we were dealing with. She was right. So I stayed at school and had to see a school psychologist for some time. Part of me wanted the help, and part of me didn't.

My mom did her best to deal with our problem at home, but it was tough. She worked full time, and I was alone at home after school. We had a maid, Margaret, who lived with us on the premises. She had been working for us since I was about six and was like my second mother. But she was also mostly busy with housework and her own personal things. So I was not really being "monitored" at all. My mom would ask me every day how my day was, did I have a good day (which really meant "Did I vomit?"), and most of the times I'd lie and say I was fine. I lied for a few reasons. I didn't want to disappoint my mother and let her know that I had failed, that I was too weak to resist the urge to binge and purge. And because I also wanted to binge and purge, I enjoyed doing it. But I couldn't admit that to her, it would break her heart. I felt ashamed and embarrassed that I enjoyed it.

I did on occasion tell the truth about vomiting, but I almost never told the whole truth. I may have said that yes, I had vomited once that day, when in fact I had vomited five times. Half-truths seemed to work well. It allowed my mom to believe that I was being honest about my condition, while it gave me enough trust to be left alone to do what I wanted to do. This soon became the pattern I used with everyone that had become involved with helping me get "cured" from bulimia. But the bulimic voice in my head kept telling me it was our secret, and no one else needed to know. Bulimia was very convincing, extremely manipulative, and persistent to get its needs met.

I had many friends who tried to help me. Brooke's family took me into their home for a few weeks, as her mother was at home and I would never be alone to get away with bulimia. They could keep an eye on me and keep me motivated and focused in a positive family environment. I am forever grateful to her family for their love and support. Brooke and I were very close friends. I loved her very much and still do.

I was very fortunate to be blessed with many good friends throughout my childhood. I always had beautiful people in my life, both male and female, who all sincerely cared about me, who loved and supported me. I will always be grateful to all those special people, some of whom are no longer a part of my life.

The thing about bulimia is it is by nature secretive, deceptive, and manipulative. It has the same characteristics of any addiction. It is compulsive. Bulimia became like a second personality within me. There were two Grace's: the nonbulimic Grace and the bulimic Grace. At one point, I could not remember the nonbulimic Grace. Bulimia had taken me over, pretended to be me, and manipulated and used me in order to get whatever it wanted. It was never very concerned about how it got what it wanted, or if people got hurt along the way. That's the awful truth about bulimia. It really felt like I was schizophrenic. Once I was in the mind pattern of bingeing and purging, I became different. It was like I had been taken over by a demon that had a hidden agenda. I almost went on "autopilot" down the patterns of behavior where I ended up with my head down a toilet bowl somewhere. And if my plans to purge secretly became threatened in any way, I became desperate to empty myself of the food that felt like poison inside my body. I felt like a caged animal, anxious, nervous, and scared that I'd be left with all this food inside me that would poison me with its calories and fat deposits.

Sometimes, I became angry. Bulimia would make up any story to get itself away somewhere to do its duty. To purge somewhere, anywhere, is "mission accomplished." I recall times I'd vomited in rubbish bins, even plastic bags, hiding them under my bed so that my mom wouldn't know until I could throw them away. I'd vomited down sinks, drains, in the garden, anywhere that would free me from the food in my body. I'd even pick fights so that I'd have an excuse to leave to create an opportunity for me to purge in secret. Bulimia is incredibly manipulative, determined, smart, and persistent. That's why it can be so difficult to break free from it. I was completely identified with being bulimic. It held me in its grip for almost ten years.

Chapter 8

MY HUSBAND, MARK, AND I MET in Johannesburg, South Africa. We moved to Sydney, Australia, two years later. He found out I was bulimic about six months into our relationship. The first time I'd met his sister, we went for dinner at her house. I ate a lot for someone of my thin size, and she suspected that I was bulimic after my disappearing act to the bathroom, since I was in the bathroom for some time. She was a ballet teacher and was used to seeing girls with eating disorders; she knew the signs immediately. She told him of her suspicion.

Other close friends of ours had mentioned to Mark that they too suspected that I was bulimic, due to the large amount of food I ate, and that I was incredibly thin for someone that did not do any exercise. Mark started to become suspicious too. He had commented on my appetite and had said to me that I had a big appetite for a girl. Much bigger than any other girls he had ever dated before. He also commented on my "toilet activity" and even gave me the nickname of "Mrs. Toilet," because I always needed to go to the bathroom. At the time I was working for my grandpa as a sales rep on the road, and every time Mark called me I was "in the toilet." He made jokes, saying, "I always seem to catch you with your pants down!" Meanwhile, he always caught me with my head down the toilet bowl!

I tried to hide my bulimia from him as long as I could. But he confronted me one day while sitting in the bath. He told me what his sister had said to him and the concerns our friends had. At first I denied it, but he put two and two together about how much I always ate and how often I was always in the bathroom, with the door locked. And I was a size 8, which was skinny considering the amount of food I ate. After I listened to his concerns for a while, he seemed to really care, and for a moment I cared about myself too. For a moment, I wanted to help myself. I admitted to being bulimic. For a moment, I felt free! It felt really good to be honest. I felt relief that I didn't have to carry this burden on my own and that my partner was going to help me become "normal" again.

Mark and I had a fiery relationship. When we met, I was hanging around with a crowd heading for deep trouble. It was probably one of my darkest times. Charlie and I were best friends again, and we were reckless and not taking very good care of ourselves. Mark and I were attracted to each other in a very intense way. Mark felt Charlie was a bad influence on me and was going to take me down with her. One day, after he found out that we had lied to him, he had had enough. Mark gave me an ultimatum. I had to choose between Charlie and him. It was a tough decision, but I knew I needed to be rescued from the place I was heading to with Charlie. I chose Mark, and I let her know. Charlie and I lost contact.

The months that followed were challenging. We had many obstacles to overcome, my bulimia being one of them. We had a lot to learn about each other. The future was very uncertain. We were taking it one day at a time. When we were good together, we were great, but when things were not good, we hurt each other with mean and careless words and actions. Our relationship could have been described as an emotional roller coaster. We loved each other, and yet we hurt one another. We were almost obsessed with each other. We couldn't live with or without each other. It was a vicious circle.

We knew we had to make some positive changes for our relationship to improve. We were committed, and we knew we wanted it to work. We both brought our own issues into the relationship. There was a whole lot of work to be done.

The reason I am bringing in my relationship with Mark and its circumstances is that the environment that you are in has a huge influence on bulimia. At that time in our relationship, the type of environment that I was in was a perfect breeding ground for bulimia to continue. I was almost always feeling guilty about something. I felt I was not good enough in my relationship. I was not at a point where I felt confident enough to help myself. I didn't understand bulimia enough, and Mark most certainly needed to understand it more and learn more about it. It was a vicious circle, though, because I knew that if I was not bulimic, my relationship would improve, but I needed my relationship to improve for me to feel secure and confident enough to face bulimia. I was scared! I felt alone.

Chapter 9

THE WHOLE TIME, MY BULIMIA WAS like a little devil sitting on my shoulder, whispering in my ear, "You still need me, Grace, I can console you, make you feel full and loved, you can indulge yourself anytime, anywhere, and as much as you like and never have to bear the consequences, you don't need anyone or anything else, you never need to feel pain or guilt, whenever you need me, I'll be there, and remember you'll always be thin with me in your life!" Bulimia was extremely manipulative and convincing.

Part of me knew I needed to face bulimia and put a stop to it. But part of me didn't want to. I wasn't ready. I was too scared to face life without it. Bulimia understood me so well. It absorbed all my emotions, especially my pain, and indulged my appetite for feeling fulfilled. I didn't feel alone, most of the time. But it wasn't as much fun now that people knew. My family knew, my friends knew, my work knew. It felt shameful that people knew I had bulimia. Things also became a little trickier. I had to become sneaky and deceptive to indulge my bulimia. I started to lie more about where I was and where I was going to, to make time to binge and purge, alone somewhere. It could have been on the way to work or on the way home from work. I'd lie about what I ate and how much I ate. I'd find an excuse to go the shops on my own, anything that would give me an opportunity to eat as much as I could of any food that I could find, and then find somewhere to vomit.

My fear of being fat (which in my mind was any sign of "meat on my bones") was deeply entrenched in me now, as I had become completely identified with and addicted to being thin. The only food I'd keep down if I had to was something very healthy that was not fattening (fruits and vegetables mostly). Any food that had a fat content would put me in a state of panic (perhaps not visible to others), and I'd be in search of a place to vomit. If we had people over at our home, I would often dish a large plate of food up for myself, but only eat a small portion of it and put the rest in a container to take to work the next day for lunch, where I would have the "freedom" to eat and purge away from monitoring eyes at home. This pattern had become part my life. It was obvious to Mark what I was doing, and he did confront me about it. But I denied it and pretended I had no intention of doing what I was actually doing.

But the truth was becoming obvious. My hidden agendas were becoming uncovered. My nervousness and anxiety were becoming obvious. My teeth were starting to discolour from all the stomach acid after vomiting so many times a day. I was consuming copious amounts of sugary foods and drinks. My eyes were always red from the strain of vomiting. My skin had continuous breakouts from my unhealthy eating habits and the high acidity in my body. My eyes were dull, hidden behind a pretentious smile that everything was okay and that I was happy. I was only fooling myself.

I seemed happy with bowls of delicious food spread out in front of me waiting to be relished. I felt excited at the beginning of a binge cycle. The first few bowls of cereal, packets of crisps, or slices of bread packed with butter and cheese tasted like heaven. But by the time I had gotten to the end of the loaf, or the third bag of chips and biscuits, it was not so enjoyable. But I continued to stuff food down, drinking bottles of lemonade or Coke to wash everything down so that it made it easier to vomit at the end. Until I reached the point where I felt like my stomach was literally going to burst, and I knew I had to desperately empty it before I died from "food abuse."

Then suddenly I felt dreadful, not just physically but emotionally too. I felt panic about the enormous amounts of food stuffed into my stomach. I knew I could relieve myself of that. But the guilt of knowing how disgusting I was, for eating like such a pig, was so intense. I'd look in the mirror with disgust, looking deep into my eyes and cursing myself for being so pathetic. I'd look into my eyes and say, "Grace, you are pathetic, you are a loser, you are worthless, you are disgusting, you are a liar, you are a cheat, and you are a waste of space." And then I'd vomit, sometimes for up to twenty minutes, to make sure I'd gotten rid of every trace of food left in my stomach. Once I'd vomited the bile from my stomach, I knew my stomach was now empty. I felt relief that the vomiting was over, for this session. I'd look in the mirror and look deep into my bulging, red, watery eyes with the burn of acid at the back of my throat, and say, "You are so ugly, I am so disappointed in you, and I hate you!" And then I'd walk out the bathroom, wherever I was, put a smile on my face, and pretend to the world that I was happy and content with my life.

Once again, I would be back on my healthy diet, telling myself that this time I will stick with it. "I won't give in to my cravings and the urge to binge this time." But as the day goes on, my willpower weakens. All I can think about is food. Finally, I decide to give in to the urge to binge. I can't control myself any longer, and at this point I don't want to. So I buy the biggest bag of chips and a block of cheese, inhaling it within a matter of minutes. Then it's on to whatever I can find in the kitchen: Muesli bars, a loaf of bread and butter, cereal and milk, chocolate bars, or leftovers from the fridge. After about an hour of bingeing, I am so stuffed that my stomach feels like it is going to burst. Disgusted with myself, once again, and terrified by the thousands of calories that I have consumed, I make a run for the bathroom, to vomit. Afterward, I step on the scale to make sure I have not gained any weight. I vow to start my diet again tomorrow. Tomorrow, it will be different.

Chapter 10

MARK AND I MOVED TO SYDNEY just before my twenty-first birthday. We were engaged to be married, and we had mixed emotions about leaving South Africa. We were excited about our new adventure and were looking forward to starting a new life together, leaving behind any remnants of a negative and jaded past. But we knew we needed to move away from people who judged us. We had the chance to rebuild ourselves, our relationship, and our life. It seemed a perfect opportunity for both of us.

Mark had family in Sydney, which made the move a little less daunting, but the pain of leaving my mom behind was excruciating. All my life it had been just my mom and me, through thick and thin. She was my best friend, she was my everything. I love her more than anything! Leaving my mom in South Africa to start my new life was one of the hardest things I have ever done. At the time, the decision to follow my heart, to follow Mark, seemed easy before we left. I knew part of me was running away from my problems, and I thought starting a new life, creating a new identity, would be the solution. But it wasn't. The guilt of abandoning my mom was almost unbearable. I felt deep emotional pain being so far away from her, and my grandma and the rest of my family. I had left my friends behind too. My whole support structure was thousands of miles away! I was heartbroken and lost. Mark and I had each other, but I still felt alone.

Bulimia was the one thing I knew that comforted me; it took my pain away, even if only temporarily. How could I possibly get rid of it now? I needed bulimia now more than ever! So bulimia took a stronger, deeper grip on me than ever before. It consumed every part of me.

My first job in Australia was working at a coffee shop. I did everything from making coffees, preparing the sandwiches for lunch, and setting the tables to cleaning the floors. This was all fine. The part I loved the most was that I had access to food all day long. In between all my duties, I was sneaking in a mouthful of any food I could, eating leftovers from customer's plates, even taking food out of the rubbish bins that was freshly thrown in there. I made regular stops to the bathrooms about every hour and a half.

At lunchtime, I'd have myself the largest portion of what I was allowed and enjoyed my hour in bingeing heaven, and then a quick purge before heading back. I remember one time, Mark turned up at lunchtime to surprise me (a lovely gesture). He waited for me since I wasn't there, only to find me on my return trip from the bathroom. When I saw him, I instantly became a nervous wreck, my lunch activities becoming blatantly obvious to him as I stood there, speechless. I was trembling when he asked me where I'd been as he was waiting to have lunch with me. He was under the impression that I was no longer bulimic because of the lies and convincing stories I had told him so he would not worry about me. It seemed easier than facing the disappointment, the fights, and the heartache. But now it was obvious that I was a liar and that nothing had changed. Now things seemed worse, because now I was exposed for still being deceitful too. I felt like such a fake.

But, unbelievably, I still denied it! Even though I knew it was obvious, my bulimia kept telling me, "Maybe he doesn't know, he'll believe more lies, you don't need to expose your bulimia, it can still be our secret." And so the lie continued. Bulimia had won again.

The nature of bulimia is based on guilt. You feel guilty about yourself, about who you are, and how worthy you are. You feel guilty about being deceitful; you feel guilty about not taking care of yourself; you feel guilty about bingeing, purging, and wasting good food when so many others in the world are starving; and you feel guilty about wasting your money, literally vomiting it down the toilet!

Like most addictions, one thing leads to another. Unfortunately, one of the things bulimia led me to was stealing food. It gets expensive buying all this food every day to binge and purge. Especially when it's only in you for about an hour, then it's out. Food no longer served its positive purpose as nutrition for me, it was my entertainment, and eating had become a compulsive hobby. At first I stole a chocolate bar here and there. And as with any habit, the more you do it, the more you do it! Eventually I was stealing food every day. I stole foods from supermarkets, grocery stores, news agencies, or even pharmacies. Like a drug addict steals for their next fix, I stole food for my next binge. The guilt was intense but simply fueled the need to numb the pain more. The vicious cycle continued. Thank God I was never caught and put into jail.

Our conscience guides us to know what is right and what is wrong. When you have a habit, an obsessive habit, it becomes an addiction. When you become so used to justifying your own behavior to yourself, to try and not feel guilty about what you are doing, you numb your conscience. You train your conscience to think that something it knows is bad is now okay. That is the deceiving and manipulative nature of bulimia. It trains your conscience to feel that there is nothing wrong with bingeing and purging. And that it's okay to steal a chocolate bar here or a bag of crisps there. And before you know it, all you're doing is stealing food, finding somewhere to eat all you can, and then sneaking off to vomit it up, all in secret. This is the scary and shameful truth of this illness.

Bulimia is a mental illness. Bulimia manipulates you and gets in your head so deep that you almost lose your sense of self, your own true essence. You forget who you truly are, so you forget your worth, your value, your goodness, and you become self-destructive. And as your habits become ingrained in your daily life, you become identified with them, and you let them become you. Your addiction consumes you and overshadows you. Then once you believe that you are defined by what you do, you feel like a bad person, worthless. It then becomes easy to not love yourself, in some cases, to hate yourself. And when you hate yourself, you don't feel accountable to take care of yourself. That's when you choose to let go and you hand the reins over. You let bulimia stick its claws deep within you, you relinquish control of your life, and you cut yourself off from love and from God.

Fortunately, God is never far away. He reminded me, in glimpses, of who I truly was, who I had been before I got sick with bulimia.

Chapter 11

I WAS BROUGHT UP AS A Christian, and I believe that Jesus is the son of God. I believe that Jesus is our Savior. I hadn't prayed in years, I felt too guilty and ashamed about the sinful life I was living. But when I came to admit I had a problem, that I needed help, I started praying again. I was praying for God and Jesus to help me cure my bulimia, to help me find the strength to not vomit the next day. Mostly, I prayed at night time, just before going to sleep, asking for forgiveness for my sins for that day.

Part of me meant my prayer that I really wanted to be free of my bulimia, but part of me knew that I would be saying the same prayer tomorrow. I knew I was not really ready to give it up. So I said the same prayer every day, for years, hoping that one day I would sincerely mean it.

After we had been in Australia for a few years, my bulimia was at its worst. Mark was only aware of a portion of the severity, as I was never completely honest about how much was going on. But I had gotten to a point where I had almost been caught stealing food, my friends in Australia knew about my illness, and I was not enjoying the "ducking and diving" all the time to satisfy bulimia's hunger. I was feeling lonely and desperate, and I wanted to gain control of my life.

On a few occasions, I had even said to Mark that I wanted to admit myself into a home, a place where I would be monitored, somewhere where I could not get away with lying and stealing.

I needed professional help. I could not do it on my own. My conscience was starting to get the better of me, and bulimia was no longer serving its purpose of numbing the pain. The scales were tipping, and my guilt was getting worse and getting harder to bear. I wanted to feel good about myself again. At the time, we were only temporary residents in Australia, and my job was sponsoring our visa for us to stay in Sydney, so the idea of me going into a rehabilitation facility was not an option. I think Mark was shocked to hear me say that I felt I needed to take such drastic measures. It must have given him a better understanding of how severe my bulimia actually was. Mark and I had spoken about me getting therapy. I had put seeing a psychologist off due to the financial commitment. I was not earning very much at the time, and I thought it was too expensive. Fortunately, Mark's employer had a family assistance program, and I qualified to get eight free therapy sessions with their counselor. This was a blessing.

I was reluctant to take this first step, as this meant I was now actually committing to curing myself of my illness, but I knew I needed help. I wanted to get well, even if only progressively. This was one of the most important steps toward my recovery, admitting to needing professional help and accepting it. I cannot stress enough how crucial it is to get professional help. Bulimia tries to convince you that you can do it on your own, so that it can manipulate you into wanting to continue being ill. But getting professional help means you are exposing bulimia and starting to want to help yourself. It is an important step to becoming cured. Most importantly, seeking help means you are starting to care for yourself, and taking care of yourself is an act of love. Bulimia cannot survive in a loving environment. In fact, nothing destructive or negative can survive in a loving environment! This is probably the most valuable lesson I have learned through my trials and tribulations.

It is amazing in life how when you have a problem, the answer can be staring you in the face, but until you are ready to see it, you are blinded by what's consuming you. One of my favourite songs of all time has always been "The Greatest Love of All" by Whitney Houston. If you know the song, you will also know that "learning to love yourself is the greatest love of all." This could not be closer to the truth for me. Learning to love myself has been a continuous journey and is much easier said than done. I have always been my own worst enemy with the need to carry some form of guilt around for something I should have or should not have done. It has been very exhausting and destructive. Bulimia is fueled by a guilt-ridden environment and various other forms of negative emotional conditions.

Some of my biggest mistakes were confusing love for something else. I would spend time worrying about myself and my bulimia and thought if I was worrying, it meant that I cared. But worry is a negative emotional attachment; it is destructive and strengthened bulimia's grip on me. Care, on the other hand, is a positive, constructive act of love, and caring for myself in any way meant I loved myself, and by loving myself, I weakened bulimia's hold over me.

Love is unconditional. I had to learn to love myself unconditionally in every way and in everything that I did. I learned that the only way bulimia dies is through faith and love.

Through finding my faith in God, I found love. Love is the jewel in the soul of the human spirit.

Chapter 12

I REMEMBER FEELING SCARED ON MY first day of therapy. But I also felt subtle excitement. I had made it here! My therapist, Dr. Samuel, was a little man, calm and gentle. He was not intimidating at all. I felt vulnerable. He asked why I was there, and I explained I was bulimic and needed professional help. I told him I'd battled with it for many years and tried to help myself but could not seem to beat it. I did not have the solution and knew I needed to start taking care of myself. I was concerned about my health, scared of losing my teeth, and scared that I would land up in jail for theft!

I gave him a brief summary of myself and my childhood. I told him I was an only child, my mom brought me up on her own, and I never knew my father, through his choice. He asked about any childhood memories that I had, if there were any that stood out as significant experiences or moments, good or bad. I mentioned a few. The hour flew past. At the end of the session, he said that we could solve this problem together, but it was going to take time. I wanted to know how much time. Dr. Samuel said that depended on me. Everyone was different. For some, it happened overnight, with a firm and serious irrevocable decision to put an end to it. For some, it took years of therapy to be cured, and for some, it never ended, as they died from bulimia. I felt anxious. I desperately wanted to be healed, magically, overnight, but deep within, I knew that it was probably going to take time. I was hoping not years, but maybe weeks. I definitely knew I could not allow myself to die from this disease. I was hopeful.

Dr. Samuel handed me a little blue card at the end of our first session. He had written something on each side. He asked me to read it, and asked if I understood it. He wanted my interpretation of it. I wasn't sure what it meant. It seemed obvious, but I couldn't put my finger on it. He said I should keep the card with me and read it whenever I wanted to. When it made sense to me, I should let him know what I thought.

On one side, the card read "The thing about bulimia is, it gives me permission to be as undisciplined as I like and to eat with reckless abandon." The other side of the card read "The truth is that no matter how much I eat or how often I purge, it will never fill the emptiness I feel inside where love should have been." I carried this card with me everywhere, trying to make sense of it, hoping that one day I would understand the meaning of it and that when I did, it would miraculously heal my bulimia.

But it meant different things to me at different times. I was frustrated by my confusion. It seemed so simple, like the answer was staring me right in the face.

Dr. Samuel told me he thought I'd need a few sessions as there was a lot for him (us) to understand about my condition. We agreed to meet every week, as he wanted to see the progress I had made from the recommendations he'd made. The first thing I had to do was keep a food journal. I needed to become accountable for what I ate. I also needed to become aware of how I felt when I ate certain foods. I had to take note of my emotions when I decided to binge. I needed to become aware of what my triggers were. I had a number of triggers; certain emotions triggered a binge, or certain foods triggered a binge, certain environments and patterns; eventually, I was analyzing everything!

I was starting to learn a lot about my illness and understand it much better. It felt good. It made me feel like I was gaining a little control, gaining a little power back in my life.

An addiction is an extremely powerful force fueled by repetitive habits that develop into patterns that become ingrained into your psyche. These addictions are fueled by your lifestyle and circumstances, your environment, your relationships, your behavior, and your thoughts. You get so consumed by your addiction that you become identified with it and almost become unaware of it; that's why most addicts are in denial about their addictions at first.

But there are always glimpses of freedom from your addiction, little glimmers of hope sent from God to remind you that you need to search for that truth, and these glimpses lift the veil of deception that covers your being.

One of the side effects of bulimia is weight loss. Bulimia can often seem to start from an insecurity about becoming fat, but its root cause is very rarely the fear of being fat. But becoming thin, and getting used to always being thin, no matter what you eat, is addictive. This was another reason that made it extremely difficult for me to want to be free of bulimia. I got so used to being skinny that I felt uncomfortable with the slightest amount of meat on my bones. This addiction to being thin becomes an obsession too. It did not help that I was often complimented on my thin figure, from strangers, friends, and even Mark. Without them realizing it, they were unconscious allies to my bulimia. Bulimia would then say to me, "See, Grace, they all like you this way."

Bulimia made me extremely self-conscious about my body. It was constantly in my head, talking about what I looked like when I looked at myself in the mirror, distorting what I saw.

For fun, bulimia sometimes challenged me to see how much weight I could lose in record time. It became a kind of game. I would weigh myself many times a day. I'd often weigh myself before and then after a binge, to make sure that I did not leave any food behind that would be responsible for me gaining weight. I would get so excited if I weighed less after a session" than before. I'd use food markers in my stomach for the start of a binge, so that when I got to purging those particular foods out, I knew I was almost at the end of emptying my stomach completely, although vomiting bile was usually the best indication that there was no food left. Markers were often things like tomato juice or a particular cereal, sometimes even fruit, usually something healthy, just in case some of that food got digested and absorbed before I got to purging it out.

Can you imagine what stress this cycle of bingeing and purging puts on the human body? The continuous production of bile puts a major strain on your gall bladder. Your stomach has to produce copious amounts of acid to break down the vast amounts of food that you consume on a daily basis. The strain from ferocious vomiting several times a day puts a lot of strain on your heart. The lining of your throat is continually coated with acid. The enamel from your teeth wears away from all the consumption of sugar and acid. Your skin and body are dehydrated from constantly being depleted of nourishment. Your digestive system is constantly under high stress, constantly getting signals to digest huge amounts of food but then not being nourished at all. Totally ironic! My health was at a high risk, and I needed help desperately.

My sessions with Dr. Samuel continued, although I had cancelled a few, either because I had not done my homework or because I had not really made any progress from bingeing and purging. Sometimes, I'd postpone a session for either a week or two, hopeful that I'd make progress in that time.

When we met, we'd talked about the triggers I had identified and the food diary I had kept. It definitely made me more aware of what I was doing on a daily basis, and I started to feel accountable, even if only slightly, because I was thinking about what I was doing, rather than just running on autopilot. I worked out my food triggers, which basically included anything unhealthy, as well as carbohydrates and meat, nuts and cheese, any sugary cold drinks, anything that was high in fat and sugar. I could only eat healthy food like fruits and vegetables, in small portions, to feel safe. Portion size was a big trigger too, even for healthy food. If I ate that bit too much, then I'd panic and even vomit fruits and vegetables up. I have always had a thing about throwing food away, even today. I'm not sure if it is because we were sometimes poor when I was a child, but I still struggle to throw food away. I always had to finish what was on my plate or whatever I was eating. This became a trigger, as often finishing what I had on my plate led to anxiety, which was followed by the need to purge.

My daily route to and from work was a trigger, as I'd walk past the same supermarkets and stores and be tempted to follow the exact same routine every day: buy and steal food for the day's session. So I had to change my route to avoid any supermarkets or food stores. One of the sad things was, I'd often binge and purge on my way back from a therapy session. Walking past supermarkets and food stores on my way back to work became a trigger too.

I remember doing an exercise with Dr. Samuel. For one of my sessions, we had lunch together. It was a bit strange, probably more so for me, having lunch with my "shrink," knowing he was watching me eat and that he was analyzing me while I ate. I felt vulnerable. But the point of the exercise was not just to watch me eat; he wanted me to only eat half of what I bought and throw the other half away. This was difficult. Partly because it seemed so wrong to throw good food away, plus my bulimic voice said, "You could be eating that, enjoying that, and you're throwing it away!" But I did what I was asked to, even though I did not like it. The purpose of the exercise was to get me used to not feeling compelled to eating the whole portion of a meal and get to a point where I wasn't full but just satisfied. This would help alleviate the overeaten trigger and would also give me the confidence that I had some control over what and how much I chose to eat.

I also started to analyze my thinking; Dr. Samuel suggested that I wear an elastic band around my wrist, and when I got a thought in my head, like, "Let's start a bingeing session," I should pull the elastic and let it sting me. This would break the bulimic thought pattern and could kind of almost snap me out of it. I explained to him that once I decided to binge, and I consumed more than my comfort zone or ate something I wouldn't normally feel safe eating, there was no turning back. I would vomit it up. My stomach didn't always need to be full for me to vomit the food up.

All of these developments helped educate me and helped me understand my illness better. Mark learnt alongside me, and while my confidence in understanding what I was going through improved, my bulimic actions and behaviors continued.

I was still stealing food occasionally, although not as much. I was starting to feel the guilt more now as my awareness of my illness was increasing, so it was becoming more risky. Dr. Samuel had given me the suggestion of "making right a wrong." Wherever I had stolen something, I would go back into the shop and return it secretly or pay for items that I'd previously stolen, thus balancing out the inventory, so to speak, and balancing the karma, as it were. That worked well for me and started to give me peace of mind that I wanted to start doing the right things.

Dr. Samuel suggested that we use hypnotherapy to help me, so he started doing hypnosis in my sessions. This was to get me to relax and return to situations and experiences where I felt disappointed or sad or angry, and to encourage me to face those feelings and release them. It was a safe place for me to actually feel those emotions and then to release them. I also returned to moments when I felt joy and pride and love, to remember how it felt to be happy and content with myself. This would help remind me of what it was like to feel good about myself, and what it was like to love myself. I could use these techniques at any time, especially at night, to relax and go to a place where I felt safe and secure and loved, whenever I experienced anxiety or stress.

Mark came with me to a session once. It was important for Mark to feel part of the recovery program and process, and it was important for me to know that I had his support and interest too. It was also important for Dr. Samuel to get a clearer understanding of how Mark felt and how he was really supporting me. I felt vulnerable during this session, being talked about as though I wasn't there and hearing truths that I probably wasn't completely open with on my own. But it was an important connection process to go through. It meant this was serious and Mark was as committed to my recovery as I was.

One of the ways bulimia manipulated me was by making me think that it was a luxury; being able to eat as much and as often as I liked, without gaining weight. So it made me feel as though I deserved it. It made me feel like I'd earned the right to indulge in this luxury whenever I wanted to. I assume that most addictions have a similar nature. This is what makes recovery more challenging. I was getting stronger, managing to keep my food down for days at a time, which felt extremely empowering. But the problem was that I was rewarding myself for holding out for the week, with a huge binge and purge session. This was like putting bulimia on a pedestal. I couldn't cure bulimia by then rewarding myself with it! This was defeating the point. I was still bulimic. Whether I did it every day or once a week, I was still bulimic.

Bingeing and purging once a week was more justifiable than every day, at least to me. It was, at the least, a drastic improvement.

My therapy had become my security blanket, my comforter. It was okay for me to justify my bulimia to family and friends because I was in therapy; this meant that everyone knew I had a problem, that I was getting professional help, and this meant that I had more time to be bulimic. I hoped that after a therapy session, one day, that everything I had learnt about my illness, the prayers that I had been saying, the hope that I had to be saved, would miraculously cure me in a moment. But I knew I had to be more committed, more loyal to the cause. Things were better in the sense that I was not always vomiting my food up. I could keep food down when I was with Mark and friends over the weekends. I could go for a few days, maybe a couple of weeks, without bingeing and purging. This felt extremely empowering. But I would relapse constantly. I knew when I was going through a few days of curing that I was going to reward myself with a binge and purge, either for one session, the whole day, or even weeks. And sadly I was still occasionally stealing food to feed bulimia. I most certainly was not cured. And as usual, Mark did not know the whole truth.

Gratefully, Mark supported me through my bulimia, but I realize how difficult it must've been for him. He believed in me and knew that I could be cured, if I really wanted to be cured. Every time I told him I had a good day, that I had not vomited, he had hope. But it was always followed by disappointment when I told him I had a bad day. He would get angry at me for not trying harder and for being weak. Sometimes, he caught me sneaking off to vomit or even smelled it on my breath. He would call me a liar and say that I was disgusting. We would have horrendous fights, name calling, screaming, bringing up the past, blaming each other for our problems. It was awful. We definitely knew how to bring out the worst in each other. I felt ashamed and low.

So telling him the truth all the time became challenging. I didn't want to disappoint him and make him mad. I didn't want to hurt him. So it became easier not to tell him the whole truth. It was easier to let us enjoy the illusion that everything was fine. Perhaps he turned a blind eye to it after a time, as it might have been easier for him to deal with. So the vicious cycle continued. Stealing, bingeing, purging, lying, pretending, deceiving, fighting, partying, escaping, and recovering; it was all getting to be too much. I was not taking good care of myself, physically, emotionally, and spiritually.

Chapter 13

ONE NIGHT WE WERE OUT PARTYING, and I was feeling very guilty. We met a couple who we spoke to all night, and before they left the party, the lady bizarrely whispered in my ear, "You must tell him everything!" I felt like someone had been watching me, judging me, and the guilt set in deeply. My heart palpitated all night, thoughts racing through my head; a voice kept saying, "You have to tell him everything. You have to tell him the truth."

I felt painfully anxious. It felt like my conscience was getting the better of me, and I could not tell another lie. It was like my "lie bag" was full to the brim, and I needed to empty it out, as I could not fit one more lie in. I felt self-conscious about everything. I realized I had to tell Mark the whole truth, not just what suited me. He had to know who and what I really was. I did not want to pretend anymore; I did not want to lie; I wanted to be me, whoever that was, as I was not sure of who I was any more. I felt nervous, anxious, and afraid of facing the truth. On our way home from the party, Mark asked me what was wrong; he knew there was something on my mind, that I needed to say something. I had so much to say but I could not get one word out. So I didn't, not that night. I was too tired and too scared. I tried to ignore the fire burning in my head and in my stomach. I hardly slept that night.

The next morning, I couldn't bear it. My conscience got the better of me. I bared my soul to Mark. I confessed my sins and all the lies I had ever told him. I explained the exact severity of my bulimia, of exactly what I was doing every day. I confessed every dishonest thing I had ever done. Mark was surprised and shocked. He felt hurt and disappointed. He felt anger for having believed in me and felt that, in return, I didn't have the strength and courtesy to be honest with him. But now all that mattered was that I was being honest, completely honest about everything.

It felt good to get such an enormous load off my shoulders. But once all had been said that needed to be said, a sad silence fell between us. We did not have much to say to each other. While it felt good to have lifted the load from my shoulders, I felt incredibly vulnerable. I had opened myself up, exposed myself completely for judgment. I was frightened. I was uncertain of what our future together held. I was uncertain of what Mark was thinking, if he wanted to leave me now that he really knew me. I was truly terrified.

Mark suggested that we go to a park not far from where we lived, where we could enjoy the sunshine and both just relax. We were not in the mood after the events of the morning to do or say very much. It seemed like there was nothing left to say. We sat on top of a hill and gazed into the distance. I was not sure what to think or what to expect. I still felt scared and lost. Had I done the wrong thing? I started to doubt that telling the truth and baring my soul was the right decision. I had never felt so vulnerable and alone. I felt ashamed, embarrassed, and worthless. But something deep within me reassured me that I had done the right thing. Mark went for a walk down the hill and sat on a wooden fence. It looked as though he was talking to someone, like he was asking someone, "What should I do with her?" Nobody was there. It felt strange.

Suddenly, I was overcome by a desperate urge to pray to God and Jesus for forgiveness for all my sins. The minute I started praying for forgiveness, bizarrely, Mark looked up at me, as if I had interrupted his conversation. He started walking toward me. I quickly finished my prayer as he approached me, and when he got to me he said, "What are you doing?" I told him I was praying, praying to God and to Jesus for forgiveness of my sins, for hurting him and deceiving him and not being true to myself. Mark did not say anything.

He sat next to me on the grass on the hilltop. It was quite overcast now and almost looked like a storm was brewing. There were patches of clouds in a dull grey sky. It got a little chilly. There were very few people around. Quite suddenly, there was a beam of sunshine, shining through a cloud that was directly above us. The rest of the sky still looked grey. It seemed like we were in a spotlight. The sun felt warm on our faces. We lay down on our backs on the grass and enjoyed the glow. Then the sun crept behind the cloud. I looked up at the cloud and was transfixed by it. For some reason, it held my gaze. I was looking at this big, beautiful white cloud and started to see the most spectacular spectrum of colours on the edge of the clouds. The colours were sparkling. As I kept admiring this beautiful cloud and all its amazing colours, the cloud looked different. It had changed its form and looked like something out of this world. I was mesmerized by its magical presence. I was pretty sure that I knew what I was looking at, but I wanted to be sure that my mind was not playing tricks on me.

I turned to Mark and asked, "Look up at that cloud above us, what does that cloud look like to you?"

Mark looked up at the cloud and then said, "An angel."

I said, "Yes! It's an angel!" This angel was absolutely, magnificently, breathtakingly beautiful! Its glowing, gentle presence was penetrating and powerfully uplifting, peaceful, and loving. I instantly burst into uncontrollable tears. They were tears of utter joy. Then a clear voice in my head said to me, "The truth will set you free!"

I knew immediately that this was a message from God. I felt so blessed and grateful. At a time when I felt more vulnerable than I had ever felt, when I felt more alone than ever before, I instantaneously felt gratitude and love, knowing with certainty that I had done the right thing. I had bared my soul and asked for Jesus to wipe the slate clean, I had been completely honest about everything. Because I had been true to myself, this truth had set me free. Wow, did I feel free! I felt elated by my spiritual experience. I felt so blessed that an angel appeared to me, that God had sent me an angel to give me a message so that I felt safe and secure that I had done the right thing. I will always remember how God reached out his hand to me. It felt surreal.

I found it bizarre and disappointing that Mark did not feel as elated and touched by our angel experience as I did. He never brought it up and never told anyone about it. In fact, when I brought it up, he felt embarrassed and pretended like he never saw it, as if I was the only one who saw it. But I remember clearly that I specifically asked him first what it was that we were both looking at in the sky, and he was the first one to say that it was an angel. I positioned it that way at the time to make sure that my mind was not playing tricks on me. Surely if he saw an angel, as I did, both our minds could not have been playing tricks on us simultaneously. Surely that would be too coincidental. Perhaps this experience was only meant to touch me, to move me enough to create change, repentance, and thus redemption.

I was on a spiritual high for many days that followed, replaying my experience in my head over and over again. It still seemed surreal. I asked myself, "Did an angel really appear to me?" It seemed like a dream. But for the first time in many years, I felt a power within me that emanated hope, strength, peace, and love. I felt good about myself, proud of myself for doing the right thing, for being honest, and that made me feel whole. I actually liked myself, a feeling I did not remember well. It seemed like I had entered a whole new world, refreshed and hopeful. It felt good. The future was filled with hope.

Chapter 14

I TOLD DR. SAMUEL ABOUT MY experience and how my conscience got the better of me, forcing me to tell the whole truth, and about an angel appearing before me. He believed me. He is a Christian and a follower of God and Jesus. He told me to keep the memory of my angel experience very close to me and to always remember that God would be there for me, to help me through this. He reminded me that I did not have to travel this road alone. He recommended that I read a book called the *A Pilgrim's Progress*. He thought after my experience I may relate and draw some strength and courage from this book. He was right, I did feel good after reading it.

It felt wonderful knowing I could start over again from a clean slate. I thanked Jesus and expressed my gratitude every day. But as the days turned into weeks of not bingeing and purging, the bulimic voice in my head was getting louder and more persistent and much stronger. Sadly, I listened to it and gave in. That night, I told Mark I had a bad day and that I gave in, promising to myself that I would, at the very least, be honest about my illness and the activities that went with it.

Mark was devastated! He burst into tears, crouching over in emotional agony that even this angel sent from God had not been enough encouragement and empowerment to give me the strength to stop. That not even my angel experience could help me to say NO! I still did not have enough strength to not give in to my addiction and my weakness. He wept and begged God for help to understand me and my bulimia, begging for answers to what hope there was left, if even this magnificent spiritual experience was not motivation enough for me, then what else was left?

Then Mark got angry; he shouted at me, asking, "Why, why do you have to be bulimic, why can't you stop?"

I felt ashamed and disappointed. I was so angry with myself. It was dreadful seeing Mark in so much pain. It was soul wrenching that he felt so much hurt and pain because of me and my illness, my weakness! Instinctively, all I wanted to do was to take away his pain. So pathetically, I tried to take back what I had told him and said that I hadn't binged and purged that day and that I was just saying that to get his reaction. I got a reaction, all right! Utter despair. I pleaded with him to forgive me for being weak and promised that it would never happen again. But he'd heard my empty promises before, only to be broken, time and time again. I now questioned the hope I had, once again, and thought that if my angel experience couldn't cure me, what in the world could?

Bingeing and purging sessions crept back into my daily life, and sadly, after seeing Mark's world shattered by my addiction, I hid the truth from him again. Before I knew it, I was back to the same old tricks, only this time, I did not steal anything anymore. That was one promise I actually kept. I was only prepared to hurt myself and no one else.

Our relationship was strained; we were both tired of the fights and the drama. Mark brought his own personal issues to the relationship, and we had a few heart-shattering events happen, which pushed us apart even further. We became really ugly to each other and argued about everything. He often went out at night with his friends, which gave me the chance to feed my bulimia. We both felt lonely, lost, and depressed. We were surrounded by negative thoughts and negative circumstances, and we were not emotionally equipped to deal with any of our problems in a constructive and positive way.

We needed help. In fact, we needed a miracle to save us! We knew we needed God in our lives. Mark and I looked for a church to go to but couldn't seem to find one we felt comfortable with. After searching for a while, we said, "If only church would come to us …"

A few days later, someone knocked on our front door. Mark opened the door to meet two Jehovah's Witnesses. We invited them in and had a nice chat with them about our beliefs and understanding of the Bible. They gave us a snapshot of their belief system and understanding of the Bible. We must have talked for over an hour. We enjoyed our conversation with them. They asked if they could come back to see us and if we would be interested in studying the Bible with them. We said we would like that very much. When they left, Mark and I were quite affected by what had just happened.

Jesus said, "Ask and you shall receive!" Mark and I had asked for church to come to us, and sure enough, he sent his workers straight to our front door! God most certainly works in mysterious ways. We studied with the Jehovah's Witnesses for over four years. We were never baptized Jehovah's Witnesses, and we chose not to be, for personal reasons. But our experiences with them were always sincere and wonderful. We made friends with the loveliest people. We always talked about how much love and kindness the Jehovah's Witnesses showed to us while we were in their presence. They were always so caring and nonjudgmental.

We became very close to Pierre and Connie, a Jehovah's Witness couple who we studied the Bible with. I remember one evening we were at their home for dinner, and I was telling Pierre about my progress with my bulimia and the therapy sessions I was having with my psychologist. With complete conviction, Pierre said to me, "You don't need to see a psychologist, just pray to God and ask him for help and he'll cure you." I remember thinking how much I admired his faith. I wanted the unwavering faith that he had.

I know now that because of my spiritual education and knowledge, I was able to draw closer to God. Nothing changed magically overnight, probably because I didn't want it to. I wasn't ready to hand my burden over. But I did start to develop a conscience. Ever since my angel experience, stealing was a definite no-no. I did not want to take from others in any way, and I was not prepared to carry around theft guilt any more. Being able to stop stealing was easier than I expected. It was as easy as making an absolutely firm decision and not compromising on that decision at all, not compromising on that promise to myself and to God for one moment. It felt so good to pay for everything. It felt honest, and that was the most empowering feeling I had ever felt. And like anything, the more you practice something, the more it becomes what you do, and the more it becomes engrained in you, and ultimately it starts to define who you are. So being honest in an area of previous dishonesty was extremely liberating. So slowly I was retraining my conscience to know what was truly right and what was truly wrong.

Much like our conscience, our bodies become trained too. This can come from either positive or negative influences. With my bulimia, I trained my body to almost reject food. My body was desperate for nourishment, but it was so used to being emptied of its nourishment before it had a chance to digest and absorb the goodness, that I think I had reprogrammed my body to not bother with putting all the effort into digesting my food anymore. This slowed my metabolism down tremendously.

My body was so used to the routine of eating and vomiting that I did not need to put my fingers down my throat to vomit anymore. I simply used my stomach muscles to move the food up. I could do this quietly, within a few seconds, with no strain at all. I had trained my stomach muscles to this. Sometimes, if I just burped after a meal, my body automatically started to move the food up into my esophagus. I disrespected food, and for that reason, food could not possibly serve me in a positive way. I had to retrain my body to function properly.

The other effect that bulimia has on your body is that it changes the magnetic fields in your body from positive to negative. This has a detrimental effect on the organs in the body and how they function. It changes the direction of brain wave patterns, which causes a chemical reaction in the body, which in turn affects the way the brain functions, which is why it is classed as a mental illness. The constant physical and emotional stress bulimia put on my body created a vast amount of toxic energy in my body. Evidence of this toxic energy was my moodiness and my susceptibility to catching colds and flu viruses.

I knew if I wanted to cure my bulimia, I had to embark on the challenge of teaching myself about nutrition, the benefits of exercise, and spiritually drawing closer to God. I had to learn to respect food and make food my friend. I had to learn to get in touch with my body and listen to my body so that I could learn to take care of it. If I could take care of myself, I would start respecting myself, and I would slowly learn to love myself. If I could learn to love myself, then I wouldn't want to hurt myself anymore. I knew this was the answer. But it was much easier said than done!

From years and years of looking at myself with disgust because of what I did and who I had become, I felt a lot of hatred toward myself. I found it very difficult to believe in myself. Our Bible studies with the Jehovah's Witnesses were helping Mark and me to develop a godly conscience, and we were starting to realize the extent of the pain we were both in, separately as well as together. Mark and I started to see and believe that we were good, loving people underneath the complicated mess that we had created on the surface.

Mark and I had been engaged for about four years; after we had lived in Sydney for about three years, he broke the engagement off because I was still lying about my bulimia and he said that he did not want to marry me with this illness. He couldn't handle the lies and the deception anymore. He couldn't stand seeing me hurt myself anymore. I needed to sort it out, otherwise he was not prepared to marry me.

This shattered me. It felt like a slap in the face after all we had been through and almost seemed like a "get-out clause" for him. But I guess in fairness to him, would anyone want to marry into a problem like bulimia? I most probably wouldn't.

Any addiction is really hard to deal with, in any relationship, especially marriage. Mark was probably just scared that I would never get better and that meant his future and our future together would be an uphill battle, which must have been daunting. But I think he broke it off in the hope that the thought of losing him would scare me enough for me to want to stop and help myself. While it did have that effect for a little while, I also felt hurt and angry. Soon the threat and fear of losing him faded away, and once again bulimia came to my rescue and comforted me yet again to numb the pain.

Chapter 15

AFTER WORKING AT THE COFFEE SHOP, I worked for a recruitment company in Sydney as a recruiter for the IT industry. Fortunately, I managed to hold my job down during my bulimic years. I have been working for my company for over twelve years now. There were certainly rough patches where I was not focused and not working as hard as I should've been, and I was distracted by my bulimic activities. My time management was almost nonexistent! It has now been nine years since I was "cured," so work over the last few years has certainly been very different to what it used to be. I am certainly more successful now than I ever was in my bulimic years, and I have genuine relationships with my colleagues, candidates, and clients. Many people I worked with knew of my illness either through friends or the grapevine. It didn't matter either way, as I mostly pretended it not to be true as I was still in denial or otherwise embarrassed about my illness.

I was very fortunate to have a very understanding and caring human resource worker, who is also still a good friend. I was open about my illness as I needed to get time off work to see my therapist. They were always supportive and understanding and nonjudgmental of my illness and of me, which offered me a good support structure to help cure myself. I am forever grateful to both my company and all the friends I had that offered me support over the years.

I remember a time we had an incentive running at work, where if we made a certain team target, we would win tickets to see Anthony Robbins and go on his three-day motivational seminar, "Unleash the Power Within," at the Entertainment Centre in Sydney. The whole company qualified! This was one experience I will always remember.

The first part of his seminar helped us gain an understanding of ourselves and life at a basic level. Anthony helped us grasp our capabilities and potential. He helped us understand that we create most of our limitations in life, within our mind. Anthony gave us examples of famous people that came from very little and yet made a huge success of their lives. He told us a very inspiring story about Sylvester Stallone. He also told us his own story of success, which was very moving. His examples gave us some insight to knowing that everyone has a struggle of some sort to face and challenges to overcome, even celebrities. Many of our problems stem from our mind. Our mind limits us in many ways, as we are often at the mercy of negative thinking. Our low self-esteem is often the most common cause of not building your dreams and reaching for the stars. So if we could change our thinking, be more positive, and believe in our potential, this would break down some of the barriers in our mind, which in turn would then open up new possibilities for us. To prove his theory of "mind over matter," the whole audience was to walk over two meters of fiery red hot coals with our bare feet!

At first when I heard this, I did not believe that I could do it. A mix of fear and excitement quickly set in. The Anthony Robbins crew started to psyche us up, all the way until we reached outside, and then down the lines to the fiery red hot coals. Everyone was pumped. You could feel the mix of emotions, of excitement and fear and anticipation in the air; it was very surreal.

You could hear the victorious cries of the people who had just walked across the coals and made it without burning their feet. Their victory cries sent waves of positive energy through the crowds, motivating and encouraging all of us that were left in the lines, waiting for our turn to take on this seemingly crazy activity, walking barefoot over red hot coals. The crowd chanted, "I can do it!" while stomping on the spot. When it was almost my turn, the crew psyched us all up and said that we must not think about the coals. They said we should focus our minds on something else and to keep our focus away from the thought that our feet would burn on the hot coals. We were told not to look down at the coals but focus on the crew member on the other side and walk at an even pace, confidently, across the hot coals.

It was my turn. I stood in front of two meters of burning red hot coals and watched the people on either side of me, ready to take on this challenge, knowing that it was now too late to run away from it. I was pumped, and I was going to do it. I looked at my crew motivator at the end of the stretch of coals, and she looked at me and said, "Ready?" I said, "Yes!" and kept my gaze on her. I glided across the piping hot fiery coals and made it across to the other side, without a burn mark! I was elated! I saw my colleagues that had done it before me, and we laughed and waved our hands up in the air with pride and joy and happiness that we'd accomplished the seemingly impossible. We encouraged those waiting to go, saying how easy it was and passed on our success tips, of focusing the mind on something other than the hot coals. At the end, we all felt a sense of achievement, we all felt like champions.

It was quite strange, but I didn't even remember the hot coals being under my bare feet. It was like it never happened. It was then that I actually realized the power of the mind, that it really can help you to achieve anything you want in life. This was obviously the point Anthony Robbins wanted to drum home, and the best way for all of us to understand it was to have an incredible experience that we could always keep with us. The other important fact that I took away from this was, that sometimes you have to move your focus away from the problem and focus on the solution to conquer your fears. This was probably one of the most profound findings that would help me with curing my bulimia.

The next two days, we honed in on past experiences and feelings we had suppressed or forgotten. We had to re-experience both good and bad experiences and understand and learn what limitations and fears these may have set up for us in our life. We were then encouraged to face our fears, emotionally and mentally, and minimize them in our minds through a number of techniques. We also then emphasized feelings and moments that made us feel confident and good and empowered through another set of techniques.

These are all explained in Anthony Robbins's book *Unleash the Power Within*, which I read after his seminar. It was incredibly inspiring and helpful. I would recommend that you read this book, but be aware that it is not light reading. It requires your participation and involvement and commitment in order to get the best results, just as his seminar did. You get out what you put in.

The last day of his seminar was all about breathing and nutrition. You probably know the saying, "A healthy body means a healthy mind." For me, this particular day was very informative. I'd forgotten about a healthy body and mind, and so it was good to understand a framework to work from again. Anthony Robbins has his own ideas about food and digestion, which not everybody will agree with, but for me, since I had nothing really to compare it to, this was an excellent place to start. His principles and ideas on food and nutrition are outlined in *Fit for Life*. It certainly motivated me and put me on the right track for a while.

Unfortunately, at this stage I was still severely bulimic. So while this seminar had a definite positive impact, I was not ready for it to be powerful enough to change my life permanently. But later, I would use some of the information I had learned to help me.

Here are some points that I found beneficial:

- Diets don't work!
- The body is self-cleansing, self-healing, and self maintaining.
- The natural body cycles are: appropriation (eating and digestion), assimilation (absorption and use), and elimination (of body wastes and food debris).
- The principle of high water content food: Since our bodies are 70 percent water, we should be eating a diet that is approximately 70 percent water content, and that means fruit and vegetables should be predominate in our diets. Water transports the nutrients in food to all the body's cells and in turn removes toxic waste.
- Detoxification: Any time you alter your eating habits, your body has to adjust to that change and in doing so, and it can initially leave you feeling out of sorts. It's important to view any temporary discomfort as the cleansing process taking place and health returning.
- The importance of exercise: The only way to achieve optimum health is to include a daily exercise program into your routine and lifestyle.
- You are what you think you are! We can assist our body's health with our attitude and positive healthy thoughts. The power of our minds can heal our body and transform our health.

- *Do not overeat!* The main reasons we overeat are our bodies are not absorbing nutrients or the consumption of non-nutritious foods is setting off an alarm to our body, which is screaming for more, as it is nutritionally starving! And finally, we eat too fast, not giving our brains a chance to tell our stomachs that we are full.

Chapter 16

I HAVE ALWAYS BEEN VERY FORTUNATE to have many good friends in my life. It is so important to be surrounded by loving, caring, sincere, and positive people. The friends we make have such an influence on us that we have to make sure that we choose them carefully. But sometimes they choose us, and wonderfully so. It's amazing how some people come into your life, even just for an hour, to give you a message, to tell you a story or give you a compliment, that something special that makes you feel as though that person was specially sent to you just to tell you what you needed to hear at that time.

My therapy continued for some time, but not as frequently as before. One time I told Dr. Samuel that I thought I understood my blue card. I said to him that I thought it must have meant that the love that was missing must have been from my mom and that I felt that she had been an unfit mother. I said that I felt she had not loved me as much as she could have and that it must have been her fault I became bulimic because she was not always there for me. Dr. Samuel asked me if I was sure I felt this way. I said yes, it seemed to make sense. I was so desperate to find a cause for my illness, to find something or someone to blame, that my mother seemed the easiest and most obvious reason.

Dr. Samuel suggested that I write her a letter, describing my feelings about everything, and invite a response from her. I looked for anything that I was upset with her about in my childhood and threw it at her. I blamed her for every problem and unhappiness I had ever had and told her that she was an unfit mother and that she was responsible for what I had become today. I wanted her to know that I was a product of her upbringing and her mistakes. I was quite ruthless and vicious in my accusations, as I was sure this was all her fault. I was still not prepared to take the responsibility for my actions.

At the time, it felt like I was doing the right thing and that it made sense that my mom was to blame. I loved her dearly, but at the time a sense of anger came over me, and I felt like I was a victim of her mistakes. That was why I was the way I was. Bulimia loved pointing fingers and turning the blame and attention away from itself and putting someone else's faults in the spotlight, making it right and others wrong. It made bulimia's ego feel inflated, and bulimia loved it. The blaming game seemed to fuel emotions of anger, resentment, bitterness, and callousness, and before I knew it, I had written this letter of cruelty to my wonderful mother, making her feel like she had never loved me or cared for me the way a mother should. Sadly, I believed it.

Dr. Samuel read the letter and asked me if that was how I really felt and if I felt comfortable sending her the letter. I said yes. So I posted the letter and prepared my mom to expect the letter that Dr. Samuel had suggested I write. I told her that there were a few issues that I felt I needed to confront her about and that I needed to face my feelings about a few things in my childhood. I needed to face my feelings from the past to help me with my bulimia. She was happy that I was doing this if it meant it would help cure me. She said she would keep an eye out for the letter and respond to it, as I had requested.

My expectations were that my mother would agree with my viewpoints and accept the blame and responsibility for what my life had become and that she would reply back with a huge apology, and that would make things all better. I expected her to take accountability for my mistakes, and I had good reason to expect that from her. I thought I had a valid excuse for how I had turned out and for the mistakes I had made. I waited in anticipation to get her reply.

The day I received her letter, I was quite excited, as I expected that this was going to be a pivotal moment in the curing of my bulimia. I was going to be freed from taking accountability for my own actions, and I could safely say I was a victim of bad parenting and my unfortunate childhood (which, you may recall from the beginning of this book, was not so unfortunate at all). Well, was I positively mistaken!

As I started reading her letter, a feeling of total panic came over me. This was not the response I was expecting! My mom refused to take the blame for who I had become. She emphasized how much she has always loved me and how she did her best to provide a loving, safe, honest, and open environment for me to grow up in. She reiterated the values and principles she had instilled in me and the choices we both had to make. She apologized for things that had happened in my childhood that may have embarrassed me. She admitted to not being perfect and again apologized that she could not live up to my expectations all the time. She explained her circumstances during my childhood and said how difficult it was for her being a single parent, with a single income, and how she also felt sad having to miss important moments of mine (and hers) as she had to work. She made me put myself in her shoes for a moment so that I could understand how things must have been for her at the time.

She understood and empathized with my fear of being fat, as she had battled with obesity for many years, and she realized that it must have been unpleasant for me to see her that way. She apologized for that. She explained that she had her own problems to deal with as a young lady. She had me when she was eighteen, she was barely an adult herself, and she had to work through her own traumatic abusive childhood and also take care of a baby, me. She also had to deal with being abandoned by my father, as well as being abandoned by her own father throughout her own childhood. She admitted that times were sometimes tough for us, but she made sure that I never had to go through what she went through as a child, which was totally true. She apologized and took responsibility for the things she felt she had done wrong.

She did not take the blame for my mistakes and did not take responsibility for my actions. She put the accountability back on me. She said she was hurt by the things I had said about her, especially my accusation of her being an unfit mother. She reassured me that she loved me with all her heart. She had done her best to bring me up with love and care and good values, and she said that what I decided to do with that was my responsibility. She said she was disappointed that I had done the things I'd done throughout the course of my bulimia but reminded me that those were my decisions and that I was to take responsibility for my actions. She would not carry that burden for me. She would do anything she could to help me, but she would not take the blame.

I was devastated, and the picture I had in my head of what was going to happen when she received my letter was destroyed. I cried so hard that I could not breathe. I felt dreadful. What was I thinking, putting the blame on my mother and making those cruel accusations? I felt like a traitor. I knew my mom loved me with every bone in her body and that she would never do anything to intentionally hurt me. I knew she did her best. I loved her more than anything, and here I was, trying to make her look like a monster! I scratched my face with fury and howled cries of regret. I was the monster! I ran out of the house to a big park across from where we lived and rocked backward and forward, tears streaming down my face, screaming, "I am so sorry, Mom, I love you, I am so sorry for what I've done." It felt like I was in hell. I thought of ending my life.

Mark was home when this all happened, and he was confused about what was going on. He knew I had been waiting to receive my mom's letter. I couldn't talk to him. All I could say was, "How could I do this to my mother!" He tried to calm me down, but there was no point. I just wanted to be left alone. I felt like the most worthless form of anything in this world. I thought I would be better dead. I finally realized, through this unfair, excruciatingly painful experience, exactly what a monster bulimia was turning me into. It even made me turn against my own darling mother to save itself. I loathed bulimia more than ever!

In the weeks that followed, I received calls from two friends in South Africa, my mom's best friend Amelia and Tina, one of my best friends from school. My mom had shown my letter to these two people. They were shocked at what I had written, as they knew how close my mom and I were and how much I worshipped her and how she adored me more than anything. We loved each other more than words could describe. Amelia said that my mom was destroyed after receiving my letter and that I had been very unfair. She wanted to know what was going on with me and why I'd said those things in my letter. She said that while we didn't always have much, my mom did her best to give me all that she could and that she always loved me more than life itself. She did her best to provide a loving, safe, and comfortable home for me, and she never, ever did anything to intentionally hurt me. Amelia said that my mom was a good mother to me, and considering her own circumstances (having me when she was eighteen and my dad pushing her to have an abortion), she did a wonderful job as a parent.

My good friend Tina wrote me a long e-mail. She got straight to the point. She said I was mad being so cruel to my mother; what had gotten into me? What drugs was I on? Had Mark poisoned my mind to hate my mother? What had made me so unjustifiably angry at her? I needed to sort my life out and come back down to reality. I had just broken my mother's heart for no good reason, and whoever wrote the letter was not the Grace that she knew and loved. What had happened to me?

I tried to push back on them and told them this had nothing to do with them. These were my issues that I had to sort out. But I knew they were right. What was I thinking? I had hurt the person I loved the most, and now I hated myself even more. Was there a light at the end of the tunnel? What was the point? I did not want to go on anymore. I needed to speak to Dr. Samuel.

At my next session, I explained the response I got from my mother and said how I felt about it. I told him I felt really bad that I had hurt my mom and that I had made the biggest mistake of my life trying to blame my mom for my mistakes. He asked me what had changed since writing the letter and sending it to her. At the time I wrote the letter, I believed how I felt to be real. We had gone over my views and feelings, and I was certain that this was the truth. I said I did not know what had come over me, that it most certainly was not my mother's fault that I was bulimic and that I needed to take responsibility for my own actions. I had an "aha" moment. The penny dropped! Finally I came to realize that I had to look within rather than outside myself to find the answers. Of course, bulimia wanted to blame anyone else it could for being in my life. Bulimia is conceited and selfish; it gives you permission to live with reckless abandon and be completely undisciplined, irresponsible, and unaccountable for your actions. I had tried to put the blame onto many circumstances and people, but that was not the answer. I only caused others and myself pain, and it most certainly was not pointing me to the truth.

But in my search for the truth, one thing had become clear: those feelings and emotions I felt when writing the letter to my mother were true and real. But I came to realize that the unfit parent I was referring to was actually my *father*! Not my mother. But I had blocked him out and denied him so deeply that I couldn't see him. I knew it was a parent's love that was missing in my life, but although so blatantly obvious, I couldn't see him. He had (and still has) no face to me. I had been in denial all my life about the guilt and anger I felt toward him, and only until recently, while writing this book, have I come to realize that I have completely denied that he has ever mattered to me at all.

The love that was lost and that was missing was not only the love that I should've had for myself, but the love that I should have received from my father. He chose not to know me and therefore not to love me. And because of his selfish decision, I have suffered. This "aha" moment has only come to me while writing this book, so my journey continues to find peace, healing, and forgiveness.

Chapter 17

ONE NIGHT ABOUT TWELVE YEARS AGO, I was soaking in a hot bubble bath, thinking of my blue card from Dr. Samuel, trying to work out the answer to my problem. Surely by now this card should be making sense to me, I should know the answer by now so that I could be closer to being cured. I prayed for help and guidance to work the meaning on the blue card out. And then it came to me. I had to love myself. That was it! I had to learn to love myself. What a revelation! It made total sense. Bulimia thrived in a negative environment fueled by guilt and regret, anger, resentment, disappointments, and fear. Love would conquer all of these negative emotions. I could do this!

But it was easier said than done. And it took time. After years of beating myself up, punishing myself, and carrying around the heaviness of major regret, disappointment, lack of self-worth, anger, resentment, self-hatred, and fear (of letting go, of failure, of rejection, and of abandonment), loving myself did not happen easily. There was a lot of work to be done.

Mark and I were making progress in our relationship, but we were still on shaky ground, regularly arguing and fighting, but having good times in between. Our relationship was rocky and inconsistent. We had to learn to respect ourselves and treat each other with equal respect and dignity. It was hard and required constant work and commitment. But first we needed to help ourselves. Again, I am highlighting the state of our relationship at that time, not to shed bad light on Mark in any way, but rather to emphasize the environment and the circumstances that bulimia thrives in.

Your relationship with your partner has a direct influence on the state of your own mind and also has a strong influence on the condition of your emotional, mental, and physical health. Strenuous and broken relationships can manifest all sorts of problems within each other. I already had a negative manifestation living and growing within me. Bulimia dug its claws deeper into me because of the negative circumstances that were continuing to surround me.

As you will see later in this book, Mark and I learned to love each other for our weaknesses and not just for our strengths. This was Mark's philosophy, and it worked well for us. If we could learn to love and accept each other's weaknesses, our strengths were an added bonus. Then, we also learned to love ourselves unconditionally. This will continue to be a learning experience throughout our lives. It is an ongoing commitment to ourselves and to each other. These two things helped us heal our relationship. Although we had our tough and trying times, Mark was tremendously supportive of me as well and stood by me through my trials and tribulations. He was a pillar of strength for me. I am forever grateful to him for his love and support, for his guidance, patience, and understanding through a terribly tough and challenging time. We have now been happily married for almost ten years, and we have two beautiful children. So I hope you understand the context in which I mention the state of our relationship at different times throughout this book, as I certainly mean no harm to my husband.

Mark and I were still studying with the Jehovah's Witnesses, which was a real blessing. Our drawing closer to God was about the only thing that gave us hope. Through our studies, we could see how we could learn to love and accept ourselves, and as our studies continued, we made the effort to apply the principles we already knew but had forgotten to practice. We were both desperate to love and accept ourselves as well as each other. I wanted to be a good person, and I wanted to genuinely feel that I was a good person. We made the effort to be kinder to each other, to be patient, to show each other respect, and to not have unfair expectations.

All too often, our own expectations let us down, so the lighter the expectation, the less chance of disappointment. We really started to see the difference in small ways, the way we spoke to each other and the way we listened to one another. We were having more fun together and enjoying the simple pleasures of life. Things started to feel good.

I saw Dr. Samuel once every few months. I was still bulimic, but my inner and outer environments were beginning to change. Since one of the side effects of bulimia is being thin, I wanted to do something good for my body. I was not purging all my food anymore, and I still wanted to remain in good shape. I also wanted to develop an appreciation for my body and feel good about it. I decided to join a gym and start an exercise program. I hadn't really been committed to an exercise regime for many years, so this seemed like the logical and responsible thing to do.

Some days, I would go to the gym and either do cycling classes, boxing classes, aerobics classes, or weight training. I always took part in the classes, as I enjoyed being part of a team when doing a workout; I got motivation from others to keep going when I got tired. Other days, I would walk home from work, which took about an hour.

Exercise started to make me feel great. I felt aches and pains in muscles that I didn't know I had. I started to feel better about my body, and it was wonderful to be doing something good for my body. I was still bulimic, though, mostly purging away from home, like at work, or occasionally at home if Mark was out.

It's important to see that the habitual part of bulimia was still taking place, but my inner and outer environments were changing and becoming more positive. A habit is a very powerful force, and it is a tough thing to break. But you have to start with the environment it flourishes in. My exercising made me appreciate my body and made me feel like I was looking after myself. Although it seemed like I was a hypocrite, looking after myself on one side and then still bingeing and purging on the other, things were changing for the better. Before, I never took much care of myself; now, I was starting to take care of myself. By taking care of myself, I gave myself some power back, and this power grew the more consciously I started to care for myself.

I started focusing on my eating habits and what I decided to keep down. I started to become comfortable with healthy meals that I knew were going to nourish me. I had to learn to make food my friend again and not my foe. This took practice and time. I had to adjust to the weight I had gained (which, in reality, was not very much but only made me look healthy again) and accept that I was not going to look like a skeleton any more. Again, this took some time, but I slowly started to accept my body in its new form. I liked the new muscular, athletic frame I was developing, which helped with my body image. Like everyone, I still had my bad days where I thought I looked extremely fat and ugly, but my body image and self-esteem had improved to what it had been before.

I started to invest more time in myself now. I made time for the things that I enjoyed. They were simple things. I listened to music that I enjoyed. I swam. I gardened. I made more time for friends. All these things made me feel good about myself. Making time for these things distracted me from thinking about bulimic activities, at least at home. The time that I had invested in myself gave me hope that maybe I could treat myself with love and respect all of the time. Although hopeful for that to happen, I was still bulimic. But I was getting better. At least I convinced myself that I was.

I convinced myself that if I took care of myself 50 percent of the time, then it balanced things out for the 50 percent that I didn't. My recovery was my security blanket. I was still never 100 percent honest with anyone about how bulimic I really was. It was still my secretive, deceptive addiction. I had just become smarter at hiding it.

Chapter 18

MARK AND I WERE ENGAGED AGAIN. This time I proposed to him, and he said yes, so the wedding was back on track. At the time I wasn't sure if he knew that I was still bulimic. But the plans went ahead, and although our relationship still had a lot of work to be done, we had worked very hard on mending and healing our relationship and felt we were in a much better place. We had built a much stronger foundation together, which gave us the confidence to commit to getting married. We knew we wanted to be together, and we were committed to making it work no matter what. This was a relief to me, as I did have a fear that Mark was going to leave me because of my bulimia. The year leading up to the wedding was very exciting. We decided to get married in Johannesburg, since most of our family and friends were there. It was sad that most of our Australian friends could not make it, but of course with the cost involved, we understood.

I was determined to try and beat bulimia before the wedding. I wanted to be rid of this burden, this beast that attached itself to me, once and for all.

But bulimia's manipulative ways got the better of me. As most of us do, we try to look our best on our wedding day, and for most women, that means trying to be their thinnest! So while I was extremely strong and fit from all the exercise I was doing, I still had the luxury to eat whatever I wanted at times (clearly cheating with purging). Bulimia was still my vice to cope with all the commitment to my workouts and healthy eating on either side of the bingeing and purging. So once again, bulimia found a way to keep its hooks entrenched in me.

All brides look beautiful on their wedding day. Admittedly, I felt beautiful on my wedding day. Some family and friends commented that I was too thin, but I felt good about myself. I was muscular from all the weight training I had been doing, and I had very little fat on my body since I had become an exercise maniac. I had also become a bit obsessive with eating healthy food I kept down; hypocritically, I vomited everything out that was fattening in any way. The couple of days leading up to the wedding, I didn't purge at all as the guilt was too great, so instead I ate very conscientiously and also very little. I was good at this type of control now.

Our wedding was perfect. We had a traditional African-themed garden wedding. We had a Sotho choir, which was led by Mark's maid Magda, who he had grown up with. We also had Zulu dancers, led by my maid Margaret. Both were like our second mothers, so it was very special to us. The day was beautiful and magical.

It has been said that there are two specific moments in life when God opens up the heavens and sends his Holy Spirit down directly to you: when you are born and when you get married. Mark and I felt his presence and his grace that day. I felt safe and at peace.

It was a shame, though, that I didn't want to smile in my wedding photos. I had developed a huge complex about the state of my teeth. They were extremely worn, chipped, and discoloured from all the acid from vomiting, as well as from the erosion from the excessive consumption of sugary foods and drinking sodas. In most of the photos, my smile was closed so I did not show my teeth. I did not bare my true happiness through an open smile, which was sad, especially on my wedding day.

Our honeymoon was amazing. We went to Thailand, first to Bangkok, then Phuket, and finally Phi Phi Islands. This was about two years before the tsunami destroyed Phi Phi Island.

We had a magical time. I had a totally bulimic-free wedding and honeymoon, and it felt truly wonderful to be "normal" and to enjoy the pleasures and tastes of Thailand without the anxiety and stress of needing to please bulimia. I made myself a promise that my wedding and honeymoon would be bulimic-free; I didn't want to ruin it with any deceptive ways, and I most certainly did not want to have any secrets. I wanted to be true to myself, and I wanted my special time with Mark to be genuine and sincere.

After we returned home from our honeymoon, and I returned back to work, the temptation of indulging bulimia crept in again, and soon I was back to my old habits. Work became my escape, and I worked late in the evenings to make time to binge and purge, to get my fix.

But every time I indulged bulimia, the disappointment and guilt I felt for what I had done (especially after I had made such positive improvements) were extremely intense and excruciatingly painful. I would look in the mirror with utter disgust and say, "Grace, why are you doing this? You don't need this anymore, you have come so far!" I would regret my actions deeply, and I would argue with myself, defending myself, saying, "Grace, you are stronger than this, you can beat bulimia, don't give in to it!" But something inside me held on to it firmly. Was it my security blanket, my outlet for negativity that only created more negativity? Did I still enjoy it? Why could I not just *stop*? I could manage for days and weeks without bingeing and purging, but the urge built up like a raging fire, and when my defenses were down, bulimia would catch me off guard. Before I knew it, I was consuming cakes or bags of chips or greasy burgers, triggers that I knew would set me past the point of no return. I would not allow that fattening food to stay in my body, and I obeyed bulimia to purge it out.

Chapter 19

EVERY NIGHT I PRAYED TO GOD in desperation to help me, to help me to be stronger, to help me to be a good, pure person. I wanted this so badly, but I also knew that I was not totally willing to let go of bulimia yet. Somewhere in my mind, even in the midst of prayer, I knew I was planning my next binge and purge session.

My life had definitely improved, though. I was starting to learn to love myself. The scales were balancing much more heavily in my favor; I was taking much better care of myself and doing good things for myself rather than hurting myself and doing bad things.

Yes, I was still bingeing and purging and keeping that a secret, but only once or twice a week. In comparison to what I was doing before, maybe four or five times a day, this was a drastic improvement. I was nourishing my body now and enjoying it. I had developed a new respect and love for food that I had forgotten about for many years of my life. I had learned to trust myself around food, admittedly, not always, but most of the time. The scales had definitely tipped in my favor.

My relationships with friends and family had improved, as well as my relationship with Mark. My success at work had improved, and my relationships with my colleagues were better. I could see evidence of the changes I had made in every area of my life quite clearly. But I wasn't cured of my illness yet.

I went to see Dr. Samuel in the early months of the first year of my marriage. I wanted to give him an update about where I was at, to let him know that Mark and I were married, that I was still "semi bulimic" (my own terminology, of course), and that to my knowledge Mark was not really aware of it. I knew I hadn't been totally honest with Mark. I told Mark that I had a bad day from time to time, but that in general terms, I was "cured." I did not tell him the truth about my condition. I was never entirely sure whether he bought that or not, but he certainly didn't delve too deep or make a huge fuss over it any more. I tried to justify and explain, in my defense, the reasons why I lied to Mark, saying that it was easier this way as it kept the peace, and also because I didn't think it was such a major problem anymore I didn't think it was necessary to make such a big deal about it anymore.

Dr. Samuel listened to me for the hour and made his comments and observations as he saw necessary. Then at the end of our session, he said the most shocking thing to me. He said that he felt that there was nothing more he could tell me, no new or different advice that he could give me other than what he already had given me. In his professional opinion, he said that he felt that I was now educated enough about my illness, and that I now had the knowledge and the tools to know what to do and how to help myself. He said he would be happy to still see me if I needed someone to talk to, but he would not have any new advice to give me that would be beneficial to my healing. I started to cry.

Was Dr. Samuel seriously cutting me loose? Was he cutting the strings? I felt devastated. I felt like a baby who had its soother taken away! He had just yanked my security blanket away from me and left me on my own! You mean to tell me that I am now responsible for what happens? I am now accountable? I felt scared.

But deep down, I knew that the time had come, that this was possibly one of the most pivotal moments in my life. I hoped I could get through this.

That night, I told Mark what Dr. Samuel had said to me. Mark seemed a little surprised, but he could see the logic and sense in it. I could too, I just wasn't sure if I was ready. But I knew it was now up to me.

The weeks and months that followed seemed to get progressively worse, with my constant thinking about beating bulimia. It seemed the more I thought about beating bulimia, the more bulimia was in my head and the more I wanted to binge and purge. I was staying at work more frequently to "work late," and I was angry at myself for robbing quality time from Mark and me. Our relationship had improved a lot, and we were in a really good place. We had learned to love each other and accept each other for who we were, and the time we spent together was special. I was frustrated that I could not cure my bulimia, at least for him, if not for me. Why was it not getting better or easier? I was frustrated by being pulled back into this vicious cycle.

Thinking about bulimia all the time was really getting me down. Thinking about my problem, searching for the answer, seemed to fuel it. Then it dawned on me. Stop focusing on the problem and start focusing on the solution! The more I thought about stopping bingeing and purging, the more I craved to do it! Like when you go on a diet and say to yourself, I must stop eating chocolate, all you think about is chocolate and all you want to do is have a chocolate fix! That's exactly what happened to me. In fact, that's probably what gave my bulimia continuous momentum—my constant thinking about it! Well, that was going to have to change. So I started focusing on the solution: what was it that I needed to do or do more of to cure my bulimia and to become healthy and true to myself again?

I needed to distract myself from thinking about bingeing to start with. I had to always be conscious of my trigger foods, my trigger environments, my trigger events and circumstances, even my trigger thoughts. I had to become acutely aware of all these things.

I had retrained my conscience to know what was right and what was wrong, so now I needed to listen to my conscience and trust my intuition. I had to be accountable and responsible and learn to practice to make the right choices. Aside from it being the right thing to do, it made me feel good about myself. It built the trust I had developed for myself, and it made me love myself. If I could just focus on the things that made me love myself, then I was sure to win, to be free of bulimia forever.

I was also worried that I was not ready within myself, that if anything happened where I needed to act immediately toward a situation, that I would not be ready to do what needed to be done. Our Bible studies heightened this anxiety. I had drawn closer to God over the years we'd been studying with the Jehovah's Witnesses, and as in all Christian beliefs, we believed that the "end of days" are near. This is also known as Judgment Day, the time when our world as we know it will end and Jesus will come down to earth to judge each one of us on our own merit. The Bible says he will come upon us like a thief in the night, so we should always be ready, at our best, prepared and pure hearted for this spectacular moment. I knew I was not ready. I desperately wanted to be ready.

There was one particular night that I'd decided to "work late." I needed to get my short list of candidates together to get over to my client in the morning. I also knew this meant I'd have an opportunity to eat whatever I wanted to and have the privacy to purge without suspicious or judging eyes. It must have been about seven o'clock when Mark rang me, to find out how much longer

I would be working. He was having a drink with some friends of ours. He was missing me and really wanted to see me. In the midst of my binge (as well as my work), I said I still had a bit to do but would try to wrap things up soon. He was understanding and said okay, whatever I needed to do; he'd speak to me later then. About twenty minutes later, he rang again to ask if I was ready, that the friends he was with had offered him a lift home and they would pass my work in about five minutes to pick me up, if I was ready. I had a belly full of unwanted food and knew that five minutes would not give me enough time to vomit all the food out and make myself presentable. If I arrived in a rushed panic after purging, Mark would surely read the signs and know what I was up to. In any case, five minutes was not enough to "finish off." Regrettably, I said I would not be ready for them.

I was really angry at myself. I wanted to be ready more than anything else! I wanted to be picked up by my love and my friends, joyous and happy to see me. I didn't want to miss out on the fun everyone was having, I desperately wanted to be part of it! I felt angry and sad. This was my doing. I had put myself in this situation, and I had had enough of not being ready for those I loved. I was sick and tired of not being ready for myself. If a situation required me to be ready to perform at my best at any given moment, I could not say that I could do it. And that was disappointing. That is not who I wanted to be anymore. I was tired of standing in bulimia's shadow; I wanted to be in the light. How dare bulimia steal the light from my life? This was my life! And I was seriously ready to do something about it.

That night, I vomited everything out of me. This time it felt different. I purged all the hatred, and resentment, and anger, and regret out that I had in me until I could not vomit any more. I vomited so long and hard that I cried. My throat throbbed, my stomach cramped, my eyes wept, and my head pounded from the strain and stress of forcing everything out. When I looked in the mirror this time, something was different. I looked at myself and said, "Bulimia, I hate you, and I am finished with you. Your time with me is done. I don't want you anymore. I don't care for you anymore! You are hurting me and my loved ones. I will not allow you to do this anymore. This is my life, and I take back control of it. You have no power over me anymore, and this time I mean it. Grace, I love you, you come first now. You have done a good job getting to know yourself again, and you are a good person. You know what is right and what's wrong. Now it is time to make the right choices. Only you can make that decision. Don't waste this precious life that our good Lord has given you. Appreciate who you are and what blessings you have now. Do not waste any more time. From this moment on, you must always be ready."

I washed my face, put some makeup on, put eye drops in my eyes, and brushed my teeth. I looked presentable again. I caught the bus home from work; it was almost eight o'clock, and I wanted to be home with Mark. It took me about ten minutes to walk home from the bus stop, which was some good solitude time. This ten-minute stretch was a very quiet stretch, usually deserted and dark.

I started to pray. "Dear Lord God Jehovah, please forgive me for my sins. I know that I have continued to make the wrong choices and yet I pray to you every day for forgiveness for the same things. I know that I am so blessed and yet I still take these blessings for granted. I want to be honest and sincere. I love Mark and I want him to know that. I want to show him how much I truly love him by showing him the true me. I just want to be who I truly am. I don't want the lies and the pretending any more. I'm done with that. I am tired of being unhappy."

At this point, I was almost shouting in prayer. I looked up at the night sky, I could see the moonlight and stars shining above me, and I was shouting to the heavens.

"Dear Lord Jesus, Jehovah, do you hear me? I am tired of being bulimic. I do not want this burden any longer. I love myself now, and I can't take the pain and the hurt anymore. I want to be free of it. This burden is too heavy for me to carry." Now, I was crying and shouting.

I looked around me, to see if anyone was nearby to hear me pleading with God. There was no one there. I continued, "Jesus, please carry this burden for me as I can no longer bear it. I repent my bulimia; I am ready to hand it over. Please take my bulimia from me and free me from it. I have learnt my lessons, and I no longer need it or want it. I repent my bulimia, dear Lord Jehovah. With all my heart and soul, hear me, dear Jesus, I repent my bulimia, I no longer want it, please believe me this time. I am being truthful and sincere. I am ready to hand it over. I love myself now, it no longer serves me. Please forgive me, dear Jesus, for all the hurt I have caused. I repent all my old ways. I only want to be pure hearted now. Please forgive me. I love you, dear Lord, thank you for your unconditional love and forgiveness and for hearing my prayer; in Jesus' name, Amen."

I took a deep breath and wiped the tears from my face. I was almost home. I looked up to the sky, put my hands together, closed my eyes, and said one last time, "Thank you, dear God, for hearing my prayer."

I felt different. I felt lighter. I felt happier. Deep inside my heart, I knew, this time, I meant my prayer with every cell in my body. I felt like a weight had been lifted from my shoulders, a bit cliché but that's exactly how it felt. I felt like the Grace I knew before bulimia again.

Finally, I was being true to myself, and it felt wonderful. When I walked through the door and saw Mark, I gave him the biggest hug and kiss and told him I loved him. He said, "What's up with you?" and I said I'd just missed him a lot and was happy to finally be home with him.

Chapter 20

THE NEXT DAY APPEARED TO BE like every other day, except it was totally different for me. It was December 19, 2003. Although my daily routine was the same, catching the same bus, walking the same route, seeing the same people, and doing the same work, everything seemed brighter and refreshed. The world looked so much clearer to me. And it seemed that everything was working in my favor. The bus arrived exactly as I got there. The birds sang and walked right up to me. All the traffic lights turned green as I approached them, strangers passing by smiled at me. At work all the right candidates applied for my jobs, it just seemed like everything was easier, smoother, and more enjoyable. It seemed very surreal. It was like God was saying to me, "See how wonderful things are when you live in truth." It was so uplifting. It seemed to last for weeks. I was so happy living an honest and sincere life; it was like I was living in heaven on earth.

The best part of this new world was that I never thought about bingeing and purging. Bulimia was truly out of my head and out of my life! I was not anxious about it at all. I trusted myself completely. Things and places, foods, and routes did not tempt or trigger me. I was not interested in bulimia any more. I had made my mind up, and Jesus had answered my prayers. I no longer felt the weight of this burden any longer. It was sensational.

There was still one thing that was getting me down, though, and I needed to do something about it, as it was a negativity lingering in the background. I had developed a complex about my teeth. Every time I looked in the mirror, my teeth reminded me of my bulimia and what I had put myself through. It was a constant reminder to me and to others. While I was a much happier person, I never really ever wanted to openly laugh and smile, as I was very self-conscious about the state of my teeth.

They were extremely worn on the edges, like I had been gnawing on bones (actually, a colleague at work once commented on them and used that phrase, which stuck with me). They were extremely discoloured from the extensive vomiting as well as heavily decayed from all the excessive sugary drinks and foods. I also brushed my teeth several times a day, which I found out later, was the worst thing you can do after vomiting, since you have high acid buildup on your teeth, and the toothpaste increases the erosion effect on them. While I thought I was helping my teeth by brushing after vomiting to prevent the acidic erosion, I was actually making it worse. So the enamel had worn off the back of my teeth, exposing the dentine, as well as around the edges of my teeth, making them extremely sensitive.

I decided to have my teeth fixed so that I did not have a constant reminder of my bulimia and so that I could have a renewed confidence to my renewed and true life.

I had a combination of porcelain veneers and crowns done, which set me back almost $12,000. It took me almost a year to them pay off, but it was the best decision I could have made, and it most certainly helped me put the nails in bulimia's coffin for good.

My visit to the dentist was not that easy, though. He knew that I was bulimic, as he had been working on my teeth for years. To start the process, he had to take a mold of my mouth as it was, and then he had to reconstruct how it was going to look. The most difficult part, for me, was when they had to file my teeth down to little stumps, so that they could glue the plastic temporary teeth on until the veneers and crowns were ready to be cemented on. I asked my dentist if I could see what my filed teeth looked like, and he was very hesitant to show me, much preferring that I only look at the finished end result. I insisted I wanted to see. I wanted to see what I had created and the damage I had done. I wanted to see what consequences I had to bear for my years of bulimic abuse.

When I took the mirror and looked at my filed stumps, my hearth sunk to my stomach. I felt quite sick. This was my fault. And now there was no turning back. Those teeth were gone. I felt very emotional and sad. Before I was bulimic, I had the most beautiful white straight teeth, and now to be going through this! Never mind the serious debt I was putting myself in! I had to go through with it. I knew there was a light at the end of the tunnel.

A couple of hours later, during which time it almost felt like my jaw was about to crack from being cranked open wide for so long, my plastic temporary teeth were fitted. My porcelain teeth would be ready in about two weeks. I had a quick look in the mirror at my plastic teeth and thought they made me look like a horse! They were much bigger than my own teeth. I was mortified. I couldn't look at anyone or talk to anyone. The receptionist asked me how they felt, and I just burst into tears and ran out the room. With a huge lump in my throat and tears streaming down my face, I could not talk. This was one of the most emotional days I had ever experienced.

When I got back to the office, the girls in my team all knew where I'd been and what I'd gotten done, and they wanted to see what my teeth looked like. I couldn't show them. I kept my lips tightly sealed and refused a peep. I felt so embarrassed that I had plastic teeth! What if they fell out and I was left with these six stumps? I felt like crawling into a dark cave and staying there forever. And then to top it off, I happened to expose my teeth to one particular lady, who was known for being particularly undiplomatic and cruel at times; she said, "Gee Grace, they look like horse teeth!" I was fuming at her; I felt hurt and humiliated! I prayed, "Dear God, please help me through this!"

Two weeks later (which I can tell you were the longest two weeks of my life), my new porcelain teeth were fitted, and they looked great! I was extremely happy with the end result, and I felt instantly refreshed and had renewed confidence within myself. This was the symbolic representation of my new bulimic-free life. And I had this beautiful new smile to remind me of it every day! My sparkling new white teeth were very symbolic to me of my rebirth, you could say. I had done something for myself that felt wonderfully good and satisfying. I had a new lease on life and was very fortunate that I was able to do so.

Chapter 21

SINCE DECEMBER 19, 2003, I HAVE been cured from my bulimia. I had one relapse, soon after my first pregnancy, which I miscarried. I was twelve weeks pregnant when I found out that the baby had no heart beat. We were devastated. Being my first pregnancy, I had told everyone that I was pregnant, from when I was about four weeks pregnant. So I had known for almost eight weeks that I was pregnant, with all the symptoms. I had grown attached to my new baby and the idea of my new family, to then find out at twelve weeks that the baby had no heart beat. Our world was shattered. It was not common knowledge to me that most women carry a high risk for miscarriage in their first pregnancy, although those statistics most certainly did not make me feel any better. I felt as though there was something wrong with my body and that it was my fault that the baby had died.

On our way back from the scan and after receiving the sad news, Mark and I were both very sad and disappointed. Now we had to face telling everyone the news, which made us feel even worse. And then to top it off, a few people that we told were quite blasé about it, saying that it was such a common thing for women to miscarry, that it really wasn't a big deal. So I pretended everything was okay and that we'd just have to try again.

The feelings of guilt slowly crept in, though, and I internally blamed myself and subconsciously felt as though I needed to punish myself. Before I knew it, I had these negative feelings of depression sneak in, and I wasn't entirely sure how to deal with it. Before I knew it, the manipulative bulimic voice in my head convinced me that I needed to comfort my pain with a binge! My guard was down, I was weak, and I gave in.

Just this once, I thought, to take my mind off what had happened, just for a while. One time turned into two times, turned into three times, and before I knew it, I was bingeing and purging almost every day for a few weeks. It felt like I had re-entered a dark world of deceit and isolation. It felt like hell. I couldn't believe I was back here again, after I had come so far. I had broken my promise to myself and, more importantly, to God. I felt like a criminal and an outcast. Like before, bulimia once again made me feel too ashamed and too embarrassed to tell anyone about it, so I kept it to myself; it felt dreadful. The guilt of being dishonest and not being truthful about this was making me intensely miserable. I did not want this life again. After the sweet taste of truth and freedom, of loving myself, this now tasted like death!

I kept on thinking I must tell Mark about what's going on, then it will be okay. As long as I am open and honest about this, then I can get help, I can get through it. If there is truth, there is hope. But I couldn't bring myself to tell Mark. I was so ashamed of myself and so ashamed of disappointing him that I couldn't tell him. But it's all I thought about. And every day I binged and purged and did not tell him, my heart burned with the dishonesty that surrounded me. One morning in my cycling class at the gym, all I could think about was what a fake I had become again, that I had to tell Mark in order to help myself, so that it could stop. I was anxious, terrified, and desperate.

After my cycling class, when I got home, I sat on the edge of the bed. Mark was still sleeping. I said, "Love, I need to talk to you." He opened his eyes, sat up in bed, and looked at me. I knew by the look on his face he knew instantly that something was wrong. I just came out with it. "I've had a relapse with my bulimia, and it's been going on for a few weeks. I'm sorry I haven't told you. Love, I'm worried. I need help. I am going to see Dr. Samuel as soon as possible. I think it's got to do with me feeling guilty about the miscarriage and not knowing how to deal with it. I feel quite scared."

Mark looked at me, surprised, and said, "Gosh, love, that's not good. Yes, go see Dr. Samuel as soon as possible." He held my hand. I was crying. He leaned over and gave me a hug and said, "Don't worry, love, it will be okay. Just go see Dr. Samuel and talk to him about it and I'm sure you'll be fine. We'll get through this together."

I felt total relief that I had told him. I was so grateful that he wasn't angry with me at all, or disappointed, but just totally understanding and supportive. I knew I was going to get through this just fine.

I booked an appointment to see Dr. Samuel that same week. Something inside me told me that everything was going to be fine, that as soon as I saw Dr. Samuel, he'd help me understand what I was going through, and he'd help me put bulimia back in its coffin where it belonged! In our session, I told Dr. Samuel about my relapse. I also told him about the miscarriage. He said that there was a definite link to why I had relapsed after going through the emotional effects of miscarriage. He explained that women who miscarry go through the same emotional cycle as when someone dies. It's called the grief cycle.

There are five stages in the grief cycle that you need to go through to get closure on your loss and become emotionally and physically healthy again. There are also physical aspects that the body goes through. Grief is a normal response to loss.

The first stage is shock and denial. Shock in a way protects us from being overwhelmed by loss. While in shock, we may deny or find it hard to accept the reality of loss.

The next stage would be where we experience feelings like anger, frustration, anxiety, guilt, shame, embarrassment, or depression from our loss. All of these emotions can make life appear overwhelming and chaotic and can increase the intensity of our suffering throughout the grieving period. Sometimes, these intense emotions can cause physical symptoms like appetite loss and sleep problems.

In time, you should work your way through these emotions, and then you start to bargain or talk about what has happened. This may mean you want to share your story or that you're struggling to find out the meaning or reason why it has happened. This is part of the recovery process. Recovery is really about coming to terms with the loss, acceptance of the loss, and remembrance with less pain. The goal is to reorganize life so that the loss remains important but not the main preoccupation of our lives.

We need to move to a place where we are better able to accept loss and resume a normal life and begin to look ahead with hope, reinvesting positive energy and positive emotion in our future.

Part of my reason for relapsing was that I had been in denial about the grieving process and pretended that I was not in pain, so while the pain was there, I was not dealing with it and thus found a way to numb it, through what I'd known best over the past many years, my bulimia. Dr. Samuel was not surprised that a relapse had happened at a time when this event had occurred. But now that I knew how to deal with the miscarriage, the emotional process I had to go through, it all made sense, and I knew what to do. It felt like that huge weight that was on my shoulders again had been lifted. I felt total relief after my session with Dr. Samuel. I had a good cry and a good heart-to-heart and walked out with the knowledge and the tools once again to free myself. And somehow I knew that after my session with Dr. Samuel, I would be free of my bulimic shackles again, hopefully forever.

Chapter 22

It is now February 2012, and I have been cured of my bulimia for nine years since December 19, 2003. I think back sometimes about my bulimic years (which lasted for almost ten years), and it seems unbelievable that I was there, that I was that person making those choices and hurting myself so much. But I was given this cross to bear for a reason, and I am deeply grateful that I found the strength and the courage to want to love myself and appreciate my life. Not a day goes by now when I am not grateful for my good health and my countless blessings. I take my choices in life quite seriously, perhaps too seriously at times, but I really do appreciate the fact that we do have the choice as to how we want to live our life. I am certainly far from perfect, but I do try to love and appreciate many things about my own uniqueness as well as everything I have been blessed with in my life.

I did not cure myself of my bulimia on my own. I got help from many places. I had many wonderful friends in my life at different stages of my illness; I had my wonderful family that loved me unconditionally; my patient and forgiving husband; and of course my therapist, Dr. Samuel. But most importantly, I found my faith in God, and through God, I found my faith in myself.

Almost five years ago, I was very fortunate to be blessed with a beautiful daughter, and almost two years ago I gave birth to a gorgeous son. Since becoming a mother I have found a new appreciation for life and have grown to understand what a mother's love really means. It has been the most moving and humbling experience in my life. To feel a love so strong and definite, a love that grows every day without fail and is totally unconditional, is empowering and uplifting. It has given my life more purpose and meaning than I could ever have imagined.

Over the past five years, I have been on a journey of self-discovery. Having become settled within myself and confident that I am in control of my life, and that I have a solid foundation to build on, I've turned to look inward, to see what other positive changes I can make to my life to enrich it and enjoy it on a basic and simple level. This has led to an amazing awakening.

This journey has been a humbling spiritual experience that has allowed me to enjoy and appreciate the simple pleasures in life, and it has taught me not to take life too seriously. It has also given me the wisdom that we are all faced with our own challenges and that if we can make the conscious effort to discover the lessons we have to learn from embracing these challenges, then we will become better people. We then are blessed with the choice to draw closer to God. "Draw closer to God and He will draw closer to you" is a Scripture from the Bible, James 4:8. It is very true.

We are then also blessed with the ability of being able to reach out to help others. If I am able to reach out to help just one person with bulimia, or any addiction for that matter, to help save their life, then everything I have been through has been worth it.

Over the past five years I have read some amazing books that have had a very positive influence on me and have transformed my life in some way or another. They have made me see things in a different light and have opened my eyes to new experiences and new perceptions. I would highly recommend that you read these books.

The Secret by Rhonda Byrne.

Source: Rhonda Byrne (the back cover description of her book). *The Secret* reveals the most powerful law in the universe: the law of attraction. The knowledge of this law has run like a golden thread through the lives and the teachings of all the prophets, seers, sages, and saviors in the world's history, and through the lives of all truly great men and women. All that they have ever accomplished or attained has been done in full accordance with this most powerful law.

Without exception, every human being has the ability to transform any weakness or suffering into strength, power, perfect peace, health, and abundance.

Rhonda Byrne's discovery of the Secret began with a glimpse of the truth through a hundred-year-old book. She went back through centuries, tracing and uncovering a common truth that lay at the core of the most powerful philosophies, teachings, and religions in the world.

What Rhonda discovered is now captured in *The Secret*, a film that has been viewed by millions around the world. *The Secret* has also been released as an audio-book and printed book with more than 16 million copies in print in over forty languages.

The Secret reveals the natural law that is governing all our lives. By applying the knowledge of this law, you can change every aspect of your life.

This is the secret to prosperity, health, relationships, and happiness. This is the secret to life.

A New Earth by Eckhart Tolle

Source: Eckhart Tolle (the back cover description of his book). Building on the astonishing success of *The Power of Now* (see below), Eckhart Tolle presents readers with an honest look at the current state of humanity. He implores us to see and accept that this state, which is based on an erroneous identification with the egoic mind, is one of dangerous insanity.

Tolle tells us there is good news, however. There is an alternative to this potentially dire situation. Humanity now, perhaps more than in any previous time, has an opportunity to create a new, saner, more loving world. This will involve a radical inner leap from the current egoic consciousness to an entirely new one.

In illuminating the nature of this shift in consciousness, Tolle describes in detail how our current ego-based state of consciousness operates. Then gently, and in very practical terms, he leads us into this new consciousness. We will come to experience who we truly are—which is something infinitely greater than anything we currently think we are—and learn to live and breathe freely.

The Power of Now by Eckhart Tolle

Source: Eckhart Tolle (the back cover description of his book). To make the journey into the Now, we will need to leave our analytical mind and its false created self, the ego, behind. From the very first page of this extraordinary book, we move rapidly into a significantly higher altitude where we breathe a lighter air. We become connected to the indestructible essence of our Being, "The eternal, ever present One Life beyond the myriad forms of life that are subject to birth and death." Although the journey is challenging, Eckhart Tolle uses simple language and an easy question-and-answer format to guide us.

A word-of-mouth phenomenon since its first publication, *The Power of Now* is one of those rare books with the power to create an experience in readers, one that can radically change their lives for the better.

Grace King

You Can Heal Your Life by Louise Hay.

Source: Louise Hay (the back cover description of her book). Louise's key message in this powerful work is, "If we are willing to do the mental work, almost anything can be healed." Louise explains how limiting beliefs and ideas are often the cause of illness, and how you can change your thinking and improve the quality of your life! Packed with powerful information affirmations and beautiful four-colour illustrations—you'll love this book!

Unleash the Power Within by Anthony Robbins

Source: Anthony Robbins (the back cover description of his book). This book will help you to break through the fears that hold you back (including unconscious fears), create momentum in your life to make difficult things become effortless, and develop the physical vitality and energy you need to passionately follow through.

The Pilgrim's Progress by John Bunyan

A spiritual allegory of a "Christian" on his journey through to "Celestial City," as well as his wife and children's journey and how they overcome their many challenges, trials, and tribulations, individually and as a family. An extremely spiritually uplifting and enjoyable story.

These are some websites that I have found useful; they may be helpful references for you too.
www.sparkpeople.com
www.babyfit.com
**www.helpguide.org/mental/bulimia_signs_symptoms_
causes_treatment.htm**

Chapter 23

As my journey continues, I am constantly looking at ways to improve my life, on a more conscious and spiritual level. I think the key to me remaining cured of bulimia is to always be fully aware of the triggers, the undertones of temptation, and the signs of any self-destructive behaviors settling in. It has been very important for me to get to know myself and understand myself completely. Obviously there are moments or times when things don't make sense and frustration or emotions take over, but that's normal. I am certainly not perfect and will not always have an explanation for things. But if I have methods of handling these confusing or frustrating times, which help me cope with what's happening, strategies that have worked and been successful in the past, then I know I will be okay.

I pray to God with an open heart and ask for courage, strength, and guidance to make the right decisions and choices for me and for my family. His help may not always come to me the way I expect it to, but it most certainly always comes. I have learnt to love myself, in an honest, modest, and caring way, and I genuinely want to take care of myself. I don't want to harm myself anymore. I don't feel like I need to punish myself for anything. I have learnt to forgive myself. Now all I want to do is explore things that make me feel good inside, to enjoy experiences that heighten my spiritual awakening and that make me enjoy those moments, where it feels like time stands still and you get to be present and enjoy the essence of the moment.

Moments like when my daughter's soft little hand clasps mine gently when she wants me to guide her. Or when she wraps her arms around me and gives me a tender kiss on the lips and says, "I love you, Mama," or when I held my newborn baby son for the first time, smelling and feeling his fresh beautiful soft skin against my bare chest, seeing his face light up with smiles and giggles of excitement when he sees his dad, or when my husband and I have uncontrollable laughing fits about something only we find hilarious, or seeing an animal in the wild, in its natural surroundings, undisturbed, peaceful, and alert, or watching the sun rise or set on the horizon, with its beautifully pure and magnificent colours spread across the sky like a canvass. Or when you pray to God for an answer to something and when that answer comes to you it is as clear as day that God's grace has fallen upon you and he has answered your prayers.

It is moments like these that I look to create, enjoy, and appreciate to keep my inner peace and balance in check. It is moments like these that allow me to appreciate what a wonderful life I have now, and that I never have to turn to self-destructive behaviors in times of stress or confusion, I only need to turn to the things that make me feel good inside.

It has been very important for me to do things that allow me to continue to build my self- respect, self-worth, and love that I have for myself. Loving yourself, like any relationship, takes work and constant attention, effort, care, and appreciation. Mark and I have been married now for nearly ten years. We have a strong, stable, loving, caring, and supportive marriage. This did not come easy. We worked hard at building our relationship up; it took conscious effort, commitment, and dedication. But our faith in God helped give us the strength and the courage and the clarity to see the best in each other. We learnt to love each other and forgive each other. Mark is a wonderful husband and an amazing father and my best friend. My love for him continues to grow every day, and I am so grateful that we chose to stand by each other, through thick and thin.

And so the relationship I have with myself continues to grow from strength to strength, and as I respect myself and treat myself with care, my love for myself grows stronger and becomes more genuine and believable every day.

Chapter 24

THESE TWENTY TIPS ON HOW TO cure bulimia come from my own personal experience:

1. Admit that you have a problem and come to terms with it.
This can be very hard to do, but it is the first step to your recovery. You can't ask for help until you admit that you have a problem and that you need help with it. You should never feel embarrassed that you need help. It is actually a very humbling experience to ask for help, and it is empowering to accept it. Once you have accepted that you need help, you become open to learning and open to change. This will help you break walls down that you have created, so that you can start to understand the problem and put the pieces of the puzzle together. This will take time, but the sooner you start, the sooner you will begin the healing process.

2. Talk to your friends and family about your bulimia. Tell them why you feel you do it. Talk about the reasons that make you feel like you need to escape and punish yourself. Often you only discover the answers to these things when you start to verbalize it. Bulimia thrives on secrecy and deception, so once you start to talk about it, you are exposing it, you are being open and honest, and bulimia does not like that. This is a very important part of the recovery process. Making people aware of your bulimia diminishes its territory to encroach on, and so you give it less opportunity to survive. Bulimia will most probably put up a lot of resistance to being exposed, but be strong and do what you know inherently is right. It will only help cure you.

3. Get professional help. Speak to a psychologist or a psychiatrist or a qualified therapist, as they know how to deal with this mental illness. You need to speak to someone that you are not emotionally connected to so that you are not afraid to be completely honest about your illness. It may take time for you to develop trust with your therapist, but that's okay. Gradually you will feel more and more comfortable with being totally honest, and then you will get accurate advice and help. It is also important that you talk to your family and friends about it, but you need an impersonal, professional person too. Sometimes, unwillingly, our family and friends judge us or we feel that they do, so that makes it difficult to be totally honest. A therapist is not there to judge you, they are trained to listen to you, assess you, and advise you about bulimia (or any addictions) so you never need to feel worried about what they think. You are paying them for their professional assessment, advice, and help. Use it. You will need as much knowledge as you can get to help you understand your illness, so that you can learn and acquire the tools to cure yourself.

4. Educate yourself about bulimia. It's important that you understand what you are dealing with. You need to understand how and why you have developed bulimia, and you also need to learn about the physical and emotional effects it has on you and what damage you are causing to your body. The sooner you become aware of the consequences of your actions, the sooner you can do something about it. Bulimia is a slow suicide; if you do not cure yourself of it, you will most probably die. This harsh reality scared me, but that truth did make me want to help myself and become cured. There are many books and websites that can give you all the information that you need to learn about this illness.

I have provided some helpful websites and books available at the end of this book as references for you to use.

5. Work out what triggers your bulimia off. With professional help, this will be easier to do, but if you can't afford that, you can do this on your own. The best way is to keep a diary about how certain people, places, foods, and circumstances make you feel and what particularly makes you think about bingeing. A more direct trigger can be certain foods, so keep a food journal and write down how certain foods make you feel. Certain events may trigger the urge to binge; write them down. Write everything in a journal for a few weeks, and then you can analyze it and see what your triggers are. You can then devise a plan to avoid these triggers at first, and then later work out coping strategies for how to deal with them when faced with them.

6. Educate yourself about healthy food, healthy eating, and good nutrition. This may seem basic, but when you've been in bulimia's grasp for very long, this may not be common sense any more. You have to re-educate yourself about healthy eating and retrain your body to accept food as nourishment so that you digest it in a positive way. This will also help you get comfortable with certain foods as a starting point so that you do not feel guilty about eating food, which is then followed by the need to purge or binge. You can build on a simple healthy foundation from there. Remember that after many years of bingeing and purging, your body has become used to rejecting food and is not used to food being its friend. It's ironic but food is what you've turned to for comfort, and yet food is also your enemy. You need to become friends with food again. This takes time, patience, and training.

7. Embark on an exercise program. This will help you focus on putting positive energy back into your body, something constructive not destructive, which will allow you to get to know your body again. Nothing excessive, just something that makes you feel good in your skin, where the results are tangible, and you can be rewarded for your hard work, especially if weight gain is a fear factor for you. I am aware that there is another form of bulimia where one binge eats and then exercises to burn off the excess calories consumed. In this case, this suggestion is clearly not valid. Treatment for this would need to be provided by a professional. Once you start to eat healthy food and start to add exercise to your daily or weekly routine, you are slowly developing healthy habits. With time and conscious effort, you will start to replace your bingeing time with healthy activities that make you feel proud of yourself.

8. Re-establish your hobbies. It's easy to forget the things you enjoy doing in your spare time, when in the past, while still bulimic, you've used your spare time to binge and purge. It is important to find positive, constructive, and enjoyable things to do to replace the time you would have used for bulimic behaviors. If you don't have anything to replace that time with, it's all too easy to fall back into the arms of bulimia's hold! Re-establishing your hobbies may take time and effort, but it is important you make the effort to find some things to enjoy. This may be reading, drawing, cycling, walking, singing, gardening, painting, playing an instrument, anything really that takes your mind off bulimic activities. Explore your world again to find hobbies that are fun and satisfying to you.

9. Draw closer to God. Your deep spiritual connection and relationship with God will help you to learn to love yourself and reconnect with yourself. Bulimia is an illness that convinces us that we are worthless, and that's why we can continue to hurt and punish ourselves. When we connect with God, we connect with our inner being, and that allows us to learn to love and forgive ourselves. To cure bulimia, you need courage, strength, faith, hope, forgiveness, and love. God will give these to you;

you just need to be open to receiving them and embracing them. Pray as often as you can and ask God for help. He will help you. Put your faith in God and he will put his Grace in you. You are never alone. He will guide you and give you signs along the way to show you He is with you and you are on the right path. Do not underestimate His power and the power of your own faith.

10. Learn to love yourself. This one is tough to get used to, and it takes consistent attention, practice, and patience. Think about someone who is very close to you that you love dearly. Think about how you care for that person, how you treat them, what things you may do for them. If they were to do something wrong, think about how you would forgive them. You probably have forgiven them for many things already, no matter how big or small. This gift of forgiveness is proof that you love them. Now think about yourself. How often do you do things to show yourself that you love yourself? Do you go out of your way to show yourself that you care for yourself? And if you make a mistake, are you really critical and harsh with yourself, or do you treat yourself with the same tenderness that you treat others that you love? Be kind to yourself. You deserve it.

11. Learn to forgive yourself and others. We often forget that forgiveness is a gift that has been given to us. It frees us from the negative grips of guilt, remorse, regret, or anger. Forgiveness does come naturally, but it takes conscious awareness and practice. Forgiveness is an act of love, so if you can practice forgiving yourself and others, then you are learning the art of love.

12. Be honest and open about your bulimia, especially to your partner and family. You will need as much support as you can get. People can only help if you want them to and if you are open to receiving it. By talking openly about your bulimia, people can understand your circumstances, your feelings, and your concerns. If you are honest about your illness and honest about the severity of it, then an accurate assessment can be made of the help that you need. When you are totally honest with yourself and others, then you will know that you are really ready to help yourself and cure yourself.

13. Focus on the solution. For most of my bulimic years, I focused on my problem almost constantly. While talking about my problem was an important part of building my awareness, for my recovery and healing, there comes a point when you have learnt enough about the problem, and it's time to focus on the solution. The more I thought about bulimia, about not bingeing and purging, the more I wanted to do it. Like going on a diet and thinking about all the foods you should not be eating, all you want and crave are those foods more desperately, and soon you give in to satisfy your craving. The same principle applies. So I finally worked out that I needed to start thinking about the solution constantly, to make progress. This revelation helped me tremendously. Focus on the positive changes you are going to make, like preparing a healthy and tasty food roster for yourself for the week or where you'll go for nice walks at lunchtime or what books you'd like to read or which classes at the gym you'd like to join or which friends you'd like to call and catch up with, those type of things.

14. Never give up. Don't be too hard on yourself. If you have a relapse, that's okay. No one is perfect; we all make mistakes and fall down from time to time. Pick yourself up and understand why it happened, learn from it, and move on. You may need to adjust your strategy, change your technique, or take a different approach, whatever it takes to make sure you don't fall into a bulimic trap again. And if it happens again, that's okay; just keep trying until you find a way that works for you. You may need to experiment with a few options to find out the best solution for you.

15. Be positive. Having a positive outlook helps give you hope and helps keep away negative thoughts. It may seem 'cliché' but having positive thoughts and keeping a positive attitude really does help you stay focused on positive outcomes. Again, being positive may not come naturally, so you need to train your brain to be positive; it takes practice. You have to adopt a positive attitude, and this starts with becoming aware and conscious of your thoughts and practicing having positive thoughts. It is important to surround yourself with positive people and work and live in a positive environment.

16. Take it one day at a time. If your goals are too big and too far ahead, you lose sight of how to get there along the way. It is more motivating to give yourself small, achievable goals so that you get a sense of accomplishment each day; that will motivate you to keep focused and on track. Reward yourself in some way for achieving your goals.

17. Leave the past behind. Let it go. You cannot change the past. Let what's happened in the past stay in the past, and start from a blank page, a clean slate. Everybody has regrets and has done things they are not proud of. But forgive whoever you need to, including yourself, and let the past go. Don't let it wear you down any more. Don't let the past rob you of the essence that your present moment has to offer. You deserve to be healthy. You deserve to be happy. You deserve to be successful. You deserve to be loved. This is your life; make every moment count and live in the now, the present moment! That's your gift, enjoying all the many magical moments within the essence of your life!

18. Share your knowledge and your wisdom. Once you have been cured of your bulimia, you should feel proud of yourself, not in an egotistical kind of way but in a loving, humbling way. Share your story to help and inspire others. This will help turn your experience into a positive one. Share your knowledge and the wisdom you have gained through your trials and tribulations so that if you help one person, you will feel that everything you have been through has been worth it!

19. Be grateful for what you have. Give thanks often for all the wonderful things you have, from the smallest thing to the biggest thing. Give thanks for your good health, your ability to do the things you enjoy, your children, your husband, your friends, your family, your job, your comfortable home, your car, your appliances, your clothes, having food to eat, the bus arriving on time, everything! The more grateful you are for the things you have and the things you enjoy and that make life more comfortable and enjoyable for you, the more you will have to be grateful for, and you will find joy in everything in your life. You will hardly ever get annoyed or irritated or have room for negative thoughts. There is always someone that has less than you in some way, so be grateful for everything you have. Being humble and grateful are two beautiful, empowering qualities. They will help fulfill you.

20. Give yourself permission to shine! You deserve to be happy. You only get one chance in this world to enjoy your life and make the best of it. We are all uniquely beautiful in our own way, and we deserve to feel beautiful and special and deserving. Take care of your health and appreciate how wonderful and incredibly amazing your body is, whatever shape or size it may be. A healthy body means a healthy mind, and a healthy mind means a healthy body. This may take effort and time, but start now, don't delay to get to where you need to be. Create a healthy mind by having positive thoughts about yourself and others. Clean out all the negative thoughts, all your mental "garbage," by forgiving and releasing, then replace those thoughts with positive ones; do whatever you need to do to put positive energy back into your mind and into your body. Listen to your intuition and connect with your inner being. Enjoy feeling good. Laugh often and love much. Enjoy discovering new ways to make your soul smile. You deserve it, you are truly beautiful, and you are special. It's time for you to believe in yourself and give yourself permission to shine!

To everyone I've known and that has loved me, that I have loved, that I have hurt, specifically throughout my illness, I am deeply and sincerely sorry. I need you to know this for me to heal. While I am cured of bulimia, I am still healing, and so I have been on a journey of self-forgiveness of the wrongs and hurts and pain that have I caused. I hope and pray that you may forgive me too; some of you already have, and I thank you very much for that. I needed to write this book, first and most importantly because I hope to be able to help others that have suffered or who are suffering with the same illness, but also so that I can let go of all my past regrets and pains, so that I can release the guilt that I have carried. I only ever want to look back to use the lessons that I have learned and the wisdom I have gained through my trials and tribulations. To all those people that have been a part of my life at some point or another, you know who you are, I say thank you very much for being there for me and for loving me, for your love and support. I am sorry for hurting you and hope you will understand. I love you, and I will always remember your kindness to me.

Chapter 25

SINCE WRITING THIS BOOK AND GOING through the publishing and editing process, I have encountered a small "bump" on my road, as my journey continues. Shortly after having my second child, I was diagnosed with postnatal depression. I went for therapy, and fortunately the depression didn't last for very long. I managed to get through it without using my bulimia as a crutch. I was very close to relapsing during this time, as I felt sad and angry about my life and my personal circumstances, and I could feel a negative energy festering inside of me. In the past, I used my bulimia to numb that type of pain and discomfort so that I did not have to feel it or deal with it. I went as far as to line the food on the counter that I wanted to binge on, but somehow I found the strength to resist the temptation and put it away without indulging my bulimia.

However, whilst I have found writing this book very liberating, I have also felt quite daunted and depressed from having to relive what I have been through in my mind over and over again. It has stirred the "demon" within me and woke my bulimia up again; unfortunately, it has been in my head once again, waiting for an opportune moment to take advantage of me. I have been aware of its presence in my head, so I felt I needed to speak to my therapist about it while being treated for postnatal depression. I did have a short relapse a few weeks later, on a couple of occasions, over the span of two weeks.

I believe that this relapse resulted from a buildup of a number of factors that have happened over the last few months. The adjustment from caring for one child to caring for two children has been challenging and wonderful at the same time. I returned to work full time after six months maternity leave, and having all the pressures and stresses of all the roles I have to play in a day, I cracked and gave in to the grip of my bulimia. I pray that this was the last time, and I believe it was.

The day it actually happened, I realized it was not the release I was looking for at all. I did not enjoy it. I hated and resented it but continued to do it more than once. I felt scared that I was back there again, but I also felt like it was my right to do it and use it as my escape, yet again. Perhaps I had forgotten what bulimia's convincing voice and arguments sounded like. The first time it didn't bother me that I never told anyone it had happened. But the second day it happened, I knew I was being deceitful, and I could feel the negative force festering inside me like a cancer. It felt bad. I knew if I didn't tell Mark, it wouldn't stop. I did not want that for me or my family. I could not get sick again.

After the second day it happened, I developed a huge and excruciatingly painful ulcer in my mouth. A few days later, my entire mouth and tongue were so sore and strained I couldn't chew, I couldn't eat, I couldn't swallow, and I couldn't even talk. I could not remember the last time I had felt such physical pain. I felt such regret and anger and resentment and disappointment within myself for having let this all happen. A clear message came to me that weekend: "I need to take good care of myself." I knew my body was now telling me what I was ignoring spiritually. I told Mark the message. He listened and did not question the message.

I knew I had to tell Mark the truth, or the problem wouldn't go away. I reminded myself what I had learned about my "demon" and remembered how bulimia thrives in deceitfulness. If I wanted it to disappear, only the truth and love would set me free; my angel had told me that. I knew what I had to do.

It was so difficult to pluck up the courage to tell him. I hinted about it and joked about having bad "mental health" days. Mark laughed but looked at me suspiciously, wondering what I was getting at. I couldn't spit it out. I was nervous to tell him. I didn't want him to think that I was "the bulimic Grace" again from the past. That certainly was not true. But it had happened, whichever way I wanted to look at it.

Since returning to work, I lost all my pregnancy weight through disciplined, healthy eating and exercise. Our friends and family commented on it. I didn't want Mark to think this was thanks to my bulimia, as it was not. This, coupled with the fear of disappointing him and destroying the perfect picture in his mind that he may have had of me, or perhaps more accurately, the picture in my mind, made it so very hard for me to tell him the truth.

Mark is a qualified Reiki healer. He completed a course a couple of years ago and has been practicing in his free time. Reiki is a gentle, touch-activated technique for natural health, self-empowerment, and expansion of consciousness. Originating in India and ancient Tibet, the name comes from "Rei" (translated as "Universal," and it also refers to the spiritual dimension of the soul) and "Ki" (which describes the vital life force energy that flows through all living things; "Ki" is translated as "Chi" in Chinese; "Prana" in Hindu; "Light" by Christ; and "Mana" by Kahunas). Reiki healers believe that this Universal life is within you and is essential for good health and well-being. Healers are able to restore your vital energy and the balance in your life; you are also able to practice Reiki on yourself.

I asked Mark to do a Reiki healing session on me to help clear away all the negative energy I was harbouring and also to help heal my mouth, tongue, and throat. I lay down on a massage bed in our living room. He started the session with an opening prayer and began his healing work. I started to relax immediately and focused on clearing my mind and embracing the experience to enjoy the full benefits of the session. I quickly slipped into a meditative state. My mind cleared quite easily. As I felt the energy and the warmth from his hands sweep over my abdomen and stomach, I saw a small green circle appear in my stilled mind's eye. The circle started pulsating and began to expand. It then changed from green to a rich deep dark purple colour. This pattern repeated, and a clear, intuitive message came to me: "You are having problems with your digestion because you are having trouble digesting the truth." The message passed by on the screen of my mind and then disappeared. Mark finished the Reiki session, and I felt relaxed; my whole mouth, tongue, and throat felt relieved. It felt like it was not sore anymore and that the session had actually helped heal it. He asked me how I felt, and I shared the message with him. He looked a little puzzled by it; he was not entirely sure of what to make of it. I reassured him, saying that it made sense to me. He looked at me a little suspiciously again but did not say anything.

I knew that the message meant that I needed to be truthful about my bulimia for me to be able to face anything else that was going on in my life, for my own sake.

Now all that was on my mind was how and when I was going to tell Mark about it. I danced around the truth for the next two days. I hinted about my mental health again and my digestive issues and my weight and my messages, anything to point my truth in the right direction. I was hoping that eventually he would bring it up and I would just confess at that point. The guilt of hiding the truth was becoming unbearable, and it seemed to me it was fairly obvious to him.

Finally he asked me why I kept bringing up my mental health; he asked if it had anything to do with my bulimia. I lied and said no! When faced with it, I felt too ashamed to say yes. I couldn't believe I did not tell him the truth. All night, all I could think about was telling him the truth. That night I prayed and asked for the courage and strength to tell him at the first opportunity I got.

The next morning, all I wanted to do was blurt it out, but the moment wasn't right. That evening, I poured myself a big glass of wine, to help calm my nerves. I had to tell him that night. I reminded myself, "The truth will set you free!" The guilt was draining and distracting. I had to tell him. By my second glass of wine, we were having a deep and meaningful chat. I went up to him and gave him a hug. He looked at me and asked if everything was okay. I took a deep breath and said, "No."

I started to cry. I told him I had a couple of bad days with my bulimia, and I was deeply sorry for not having told him. He pulled me to his chest and gave me a tender hug; he said it was okay and that he knew how difficult it must have been for me to tell him. He asked how long it had been going on and how severe it was. I reassured him it wasn't severe at all and that it had only recently happened on a couple of occasions. I added that I felt scared and knew I needed to tell him to help myself. I could not have asked for a better reaction from him. He offered me exactly what I needed: love, compassion, understanding, and empathy.

So now I have come to realize that writing this book was another part of my journey. It has helped me close the chapter and complete the cycle. How could I expect to go through this entire process of reliving my experiences and not be "ruffled up" a bit?

Thankfully, I have learnt another important lesson through this experience; I have learnt to release and relinquish the guilt, blame, and regret that I have been accustomed to carrying. I have always carried guilt, for everything! It has driven me crazy! And bulimia lusts for that—it hungers for an environment laced with guilt, blame, and regret, as it adds to a self-loathing and resentful relationship with yourself. So through this experience, I have learnt to release guilt, blame, and regret. It has no place inside my soul any longer. I have learnt to accept things for what they are and to accept that I am doing the best I can at any moment. I no longer live in the space where I "should have done this" or "should have said that," but I accept that things are the way they are!

I needed to shake myself free from the negative energy that was still latched onto me whilst writing my story. I have continued to learn and realize that it is okay to make mistakes, but the important thing is to learn the lesson from that mistake so that you don't need to make that same mistake again.

So in truth, I can honestly say that I feel my bulimia has finally died. Now all I can hope for is that I can, in turn, help someone save himself or herself or one of his or her loved ones from "what's eating them"—be it bulimia, anorexia, or any kind of eating disorder or addiction for that matter.

This, I do know: be love always and thus be true to yourself. Through love, the truth will set you free!

John 8:32
"Then you will know the truth, and the truth will set you free."